A

Classic
REPRINT

50 YEARS
OF
F.A. CUP FINALS

1883 — 1932

**Blackburn
Olympic**

**Newcastle
United**

**ORIGINAL EDITION
PUBLISHED 1932**

THE CLASSIC REPRINT SERIES

The original edition of 50 YEARS OF FA CUP FINALS was first published in 1932 and is widely accepted as the first-ever definitive history of Football's greatest and oldest club 'cup' competition. Copies of that edition, which were printed with a flimsy paper cover, now change hands for upwards of £50 on the few occasions that they come onto the market and, in publishing this book as the first title in our Classic Reprint Series, we are making this excellent book available to many more football followers.

We have kept all of the original text as published in 1932 and have even included original advertisements to retain the 1930's flavour of the book but, upon editing the copy I felt that we could improve the overall content by adding a few more statistics! This we have done by including a section at the end with details of every team line-up and the goalscorers.

Future titles which we hope to publish in this series will include books relating to individual clubs and we welcome suggestions from our readers as to any books which they would like to see in the series.

MIKE ROSS — Editor

British Library Cataloguing in Publication Data

50 Years of FA Cup Finals 1883-1932
786.33464

ISBN 0-947808-15-9

© SOCCER BOOK PUBLISHING LIMITED
    72 St. Peters Avenue
    CLEETHORPES
    DN35 8HU

Cover design by Simon Hudson

Printed in Great Britain by
ADLARD PRINT & TYPESETTING SERVICES, RUDDINGTON, NOTTINGHAM.

Patron
His Majesty
THE KING.

Photo VANDYK

SIR CHARLES CLEGG
President
THE FOOTBALL
ASSOCIATION

SIR. FREDERICK WALL
Secretary
THE FOOTBALL
ASSOCIATION

Introduction

❦ ❦ ❦

THE "Final" of 1882-1883 rung down the curtain for all time on the Association Cup as a purely amateur competition.

The present year of 1932 may, therefore, be fittingly described as a Jubilee landmark of the tourney to which amateurism is still heartily welcomed, but where professionalism overwhelmingly predominates.

Blackburn Olympic, who beat Old Etonians on this historical occasion, sprung a great surprise on their redoubtable opponents, and the onlookers little realised that the Cup was being taken away from London not to return for nearly twenty years.

This victory of the Olympic Club was the one great achievement of their brief career, as fates decreed that they should soon afterwards fade out of the picture to make way for their more powerful local rivals, the " Rovers."

Still, their name remains as the last of the amateur teams to win the Association Cup, and it is extremely unlikely that it will ever be replaced by any other on this record of distinction.

Queen's Park (of Glasgow) the still famous Scottish Amateur combination succeeded in reaching the Final in the following two seasons, but for the past half century no other amateur eleven has figured in the last stage of the Cup.

Established on October 16th, 1871, the Challenge Cup (as it was then called) secured fifteen entries for the opening competition, but their titles make unfamiliar reading to the present day generation compared with those of the professional clubs now household names throughout the country.

Barnes—Civil Service—Clapham Rovers—Hitchin—Maidenhead—Marlow — Donington School — Wanderers — Hampstead Heathens—Harrow Chequers—Reigate Priory—Royal Engineers—Upton Park—Crystal Palace and Queen's Park were the pioneers in this epoch-making competition, destined in the years to follow to create more interest and arouse more enthusiasm than any other form of sport the world has ever witnessed.

The Cup in itself was of very little intrinsic value—possibly twenty pounds—and the vandals who annexed it when on exhibition at

Birmingham, after being won by Aston Villa in 1895, would reap a very meagre recompense for their enterprise if its destination was the melting pot.

In the early days the Cup rules were short and simple in distinct contrast to the elaborate code built up since.

That the early rules of the game were distinctly robust and required tightening up is clearly evidenced when one reads a law of the game that " No player shall charge his opponent by leaping on him."

The Cup was open to all Clubs belonging to the Association on payment of an entry fee of five shillings. The winning team had to receive " Medals or Badges of trifling value," but there is no record of the runners-up receiving any recognition until some years later.

During the Amateur period the Wanderers won the Cup on five occasions, Old Etonians twice, Oxford University, Royal Engineers, Clapham Rovers, Old Carthusians and Blackburn Olympic once each.

By winning the Cup in 1878 for the third time in succession, the Wanderers became the owners of the " Little Tin Idol," as it was then affectionately named, but to their very great credit they generously handed it back to the Committee on the condition that in future it was not to be won outright by any Club. The deeds of the Wanderers are written deep in the early annals of the game, and it seems the very irony of fate that the year marking their remarkable and still unbeaten record of three consecutive Cup victories should be the last of their prominence, as they never again figured in the Final Cup Tie.

An outstanding personality during this period was the late Lord Kinnaird. He was a tremendous influence for the progress of the Association code, and played in the winning team for the Cup on five occasions.

On the completion of his twenty-one years' service as President of the Football Association, he was presented by the Council with a replica of the old cup—one of his most treasured possessions, and possibly the inspiration of more happy, though strenuous, memories than falls to the lot of most men.

By the time that Blackburn Rovers began their wonderful career in the Cup, interest was gradually growing and entries became much more numerous.

One hundred Clubs enrolled for the season 1883-1884, and although all entrants were still supposed to possess amateur status it was common knowledge that many of the players were being paid. It was not, however, until the following season that professionalism was officially recognised and payments legalised by the Association.

These payments naturally varied accordingly to the abilities of the different players, but it makes quaint reading in view of the remuneration and high transfer fees paid at the present time to refer to a record in the minute book of Bury which gives as follows :—" Resolved that George Ross's pay be increased from three shillings to four shillings per week." Such were the munificent wages of the day!

George Ross was one of the early stalwarts of the game, and his name will live in football history as long as there is a Club in Lancashire.

The majority of these early Clubs suffered from a lack of finance, and it is on record that in an endeavour to reduce a debt of £120 0s. 0d., Blackburn Rovers were invited to play Bury on a guarantee of £12 0s. 0d. The receipts were fifteen shillings!

The establishment of the Cup Competition has proved an event of vast importance, though its earlier career was like to that of most other mundane things, quiet and unobtrusive.

Speculation as to what these legislators of the old regime would now think of the ultimate results of their labours is idle, but in their wildest dreams they could never have conceived the vast organisation now brought into being or the spectacular scenes attendant on every present day Final.

The names of the Council of the Football Association who are responsible for the control of " The Cup " are little known in the main to the general public, but the name of their popular Secretary is possibly more familiar than that of most members of the Cabinet.

When Honorary Secretary to the Middlesex Association he was the founder and leading spirit in the formation of the Referees' Association, and practically his life's work has been devoted to the best interests of the Association code.

He has had the privilege of receiving His Majesty The King on various occasions to witness the Cup Final, and it was a delightful and well-merited reward when, in 1930, His Majesty honoured Sir Frederick Wall with the distinction of Knighthood.

In its appeal to the multitude the Cup Final takes rank in popularity with the Derby and Grand National, and whereas a generation ago Association Football was the target for sneers from a certain number of superior persons, in our day its social prestige is secure.

It is hoped that the portraits of the players and the descriptions of the matches given on the following pages will bring back many happy memories of these stirring encounters, and provide a lasting chronicle of possibly the chief open-air festival of English sport.

Blackburn Olympic, 1882-3

WARBURTON   ASTLEY   HACKING   (Reserve)   YATES   GIBSON
DEWHURST   COSTLEY   WILSON   WARD
HUNTER   MATTHEWS

ARISTOCRATS *versus* Artisans would have suitably titled this memorable encounter between teams from the historical playing fields of old Eton and a nondescript eleven of working men from Blackburn.

That the southern team of famous amateur cracks would have their colours lowered by such a combination was a thing unthinkable—but the unexpected happened.

The Olympic eleven, composed mostly of spinners, cotton operatives, and players of humble origin, gave such an exhibition of football as had never been seen in London before. The welding together of short passes, and dribbling with occasional long passing from wing to wing, utterly demoralised their opponents, and their tactics simply wore the Etonians off their legs. Charging from behind, pushing with hands, and in some cases even holding were frequent incidents in a game where appeals were continuous, but apart from these lapses, the Olympic adoption of the Scotch system of play left their opponents guessing, and before they had time to size up the " new model " the first triumph of Lancashire in the final was assured.

On the call of time, each side had scored one goal, but the Old Etonians agreed to continue for an extra half hour. During this period, Dewhurst, on the right wing, sent one of his long high passes to little Costley on the left wing, the latter making no mistake and notching the winning point.

The scenes which followed this match at the Oval were hitherto without parallel in the football world, and when " Captain " Warburton (a master plumber) was handed the Cup by Major Marindin, the then President of the Association, excitement quite carried the provincials away. This was the last occasion on which two purely amateur clubs contested for the honour of securing the Cup.

*Referee :—*C. CRUMP.   *Result :—*BLACKBURN OLYMPIC   ...   2 goals.
                                                   OLD ETONIANS   ...   1 goal.

Blackburn Rovers, 1883-4

LOFTHOUSE   McINTYRE   BEVERLEY   ARTHUR   SUTER   FORREST
                        DOUGLAS   SOURBUTTS   BROWN   INGLIS   HARGREAVES

"A NORTHERN horde of uncouth garb and strange oaths," whose doings were likened unto a tribe of Soudanese Arabs let loose, was the description given by the now defunct *Pall Mall Gazette* to a section of the 12,000 spectators who assembled at the Oval to witness Blackburn Rovers begin their wonderful career as winners in the Cup Competition. Whilst still supposed to be amateurs, it was perfectly well known in Lancashire that the majority of the Rovers' players were paid, though the more responsible club officials denied the fact in public. No football match in the South had ever given rise to such universal excitement as this Final with Queen's Park of Glasgow. For the first time since the institution of the trophy, a Scottish Club had gone in thoroughly for the competition, and hence an International character was given to the contest. Queen's Park, who had vanquished the previous year's winners, Olympic, in the semi-final, had indeed a team composed almost entirely of Internationals, but, although they put up a magnificent exhibition, the game, which was evenly contested throughout, ended in favour of the Rovers. "Jimmy" Brown, the Rovers' Captain, a Lancastrian born and bred, and one of the smartest assimilators of the dribbling and passing methods of play, beat Gillespie to score the opening goal—Forrest following on with a second. Although Christie scored for the Queen's, they were unable to draw level, so once again the home-coming of the Cup to Blackburn was a triumphant one.

Major Marindin, who refereed this match, was in some quarters accused of unfairness. Such a charge was, of course, ridiculous, although it was very unusual for four goals to be scored and disallowed. The offside rule was not as yet quite clearly appreciated, but as of the four goals disallowed two had been scored by either side, reason for serious complaint was eased over.

Referee :—MAJOR MARINDIN.   *Result :*—BLACKBURN ROVERS   ...   2 goals.
                                              QUEEN'S PARK   ...   1 goal.

Blackburn Rovers, 1884-5

SOURBUTTS		LOFTHOUSE	FECITT
HAWORTH	BROWN	SUTER	FORREST
TURNER	McINTYRE	ARTHUR	DOUGLAS

ONCE again Queen's Park travelled all the way from Glasgow to measure their strength against their conquerors of the previous year. The crowd at the Oval again beat all previous records—close on 20,000 spectators impartially applauding the efforts of the rival Elevens. Scenes reminiscent of the previous year's Final marked the advent into London of the rival club's adherents, the enthusiasm of the Lancashire Club's supporters being supplemented on this occasion by many pipers from over the border. Queen's Park, true to their traditions, put up one of the gamest exhibitions possible, the play fluctuating from end to end. During the first half, however, the Rovers scored two goals, and it soon became apparent to the onlookers that the leaders always had something up their sleeves. Their forward line completely outclassed their opponents, but the back play on both sides was excellent. No scoring took place in the second half, although it was only on account of slack shooting that on several occasions the Scottish goal escaped falling. At this distance of time, one cannot but feel sympathy with the gallant Queen's Park, who came so far and so near to the coveted trophy yet again to fail. There is not now, and on the whole there never has been, a more sportsmanlike club, but while, no doubt, there was still a little feeling that the referee's decisions in the previous year's Final had not been quite so impartial as they might have been, it was the conviction that the combination of England's elevens had become so increasingly powerful that caused their decision not to play for the Cup again.

In this year the payment of players was officially legalised in the North, although in the South ten years elapsed before the professional side of the game was developed. The first professional Southern club to reach a semi-final in the Cup was Southampton. Arsenal became professional in 1891.

Referee :—MAJOR MARINDIN.

Result :—BLACKBURN ROVERS ... 2 goals.
QUEEN'S PARK ... ... Nil.

C

Blackburn Rovers, 1885-6

Turner		Walton		Strachan		Fecitt
Sourbutts			Suter			Forrest
McIntyre		Brown		Arthur		Douglas

FOR the third year in succession the all-conquering Rovers found themselves at the Oval, on this occasion pitted against West Bromwich Albion, who had qualified for the Final by beating Old Westminsters by no less than 6—0.

The Final this year fell on Boat Race Day, which might account for the crowd attending not reaching the proportions of the previous year. The gate was estimated at 15,000.

Any lack in numbers, however, was more than made up in enthusiasm, as partisanship for either side was very pronounced. An exciting struggle was witnessed, honours being fairly divided, but neither side being able to gain an advantage, the result was a goalless draw.

To effect a draw in this game, against the most redoubtable of all Cup-fighters, was a magnificent performance on the part of the Albion, especially in view of the fact that only a few years previously the band of West Bromwich lads who formed the Club (then called West Bromwich Strollers) had to club together to buy a football, and practised for their matches on a piece of waste ground.

The re-play was ordered to take place at Derby, being the first time in the history of the Cup that a Final had been played out of London. The locals rose to the occasion by mustering a crowd estimated at 12,000, but, unfortunately, they were not accorded the brilliant exhibition anticipated.

The game in general was a complete reversal of the first match, the Rovers taking the play in hand right from the kick-off, and running out winners much easier than the score of 2—0 represents. The Rovers all round were seen to much better advantage than their opponents, and by scoring their third successive win in the Final equalled the feat which hitherto only the Wanderers had accomplished, and which has never since been repeated. Walton replaced Heyes in the re-play.

Referee :—MAJOR MARINDIN.

Result :—BLACKBURN ROVERS ... 2 goals.
WEST BROMWICH ALBION Nil.

11

Aston Villa, 1886-7

BURTON SIMMONDS DAVIS HUNTER WARNER BROWN DAWSON VAUGHTON COULTON YATES HODGETTS

T HE increasing popularity of the game was clearly demonstrated by the enormous crowd which assembled on this occasion at the Oval. No official figures were available, but it was estimated that well over 20,000 were in attendance. Many interesting incidents in connection with the matches leading up to this Final no doubt played an important part in maintaining the ever-growing interest.

Several Scottish elevens, including Renton, Glasgow Rangers, Heart of Midlothian and Partick Thistle had entered, while an Irish Club, Cliftonville, also competed, and several Welsh teams. Only the Glasgow Rangers had survived until the semi-final, when they met their Waterloo in Aston Villa. Preston North End, who were hot favourites, had also been beaten in the semi-final by West Bromwich.

The rivalry between the two Midland elevens was very pronounced, favouritism, if any, naturally inclining towards the Albion, whose gallant fight the previous year was fresh in the memories of all. Also their victory over Preston North End pointed to their success on this occasion, but it was not to be. The Albion had all the best of the opening exchanges and on several occasions seemed to have the Villa goal at their mercy. After about twenty minutes' play, however, their game seemed to go all to pieces and the Villa practically did as they liked. It was difficult to reconcile this form of the Albion compared with that shown when they had overthrown the all but invincible North End in the semi-final, but they were doomed to disappointment and defeat. By scoring the only two goals in the match, the Villa were enabled to take the Cup to the Midlands for the first time in its history.

The Villa undoubtedly had a particularly talented team at this period and, needless to state, this culmination to their successes was duly honoured by their fellow townsmen on their triumphal return.

Referee :—MAJOR MARINDIN.

Result :—ASTON VILLA ... ... 2 goals.
WEST BROMWICH ALBION Nil.

West Bromwich Albion, 1887-8

ALDRIDGE   PERRY   HORTON   ROBERTS   TIMMINS   GREEN
WOODHALL   BASSETT   BAYLISS   PEARSON   WILSON

P RESTON NORTH END, who were credited with being the finest exponents of the game at this period, and had an unbroken succession of victories during the season, were naturally super-confident of playing this Final to their credit. They are reputed to have asked permission from Major Marindin to have their photographs taken with the Cup *before* the match, only to be met with the brisk response—" Had you not better win it first ? "

Although the Albion had fought their way to the Final for the third year in succession, their prospect of winning the Cup against their redoubtable opponents seemed as far off as ever. Inspired by W. Bassett, a mere youth at that time and destined to become one of the most famous forwards who has ever lived, they, however, played the game of their careers.

Breaking away from the regulation methods of short passing and combination adopted by Preston, the Albion went in for a policy of long passing and dashing runs, completely upsetting the more cal-culated moves of their opponents, who, while possibly having the better of the game, could do every-thing but score. The game was an extremely fast one, vigorous and well contested. Bayliss scored the only goal in the first half for the Albion, Goodall equalising for Preston early in the second half. Then a nice pass by Bassett produced a goal from the foot of Spry Woodhall and the Albion triumphed at the expense of the greatest combination the football world has known. The sympathies of the crowd described as " enormous," were unmistakably on the side of the winners, who in the two previous years had made plucky but unsuccessful attempts to lift the Cup. The Albion eleven were also all Stafford-shire lads, with a total wage list of £5 10s. per week, whereas Preston were all highly paid " professors " of the art.

Referee :—MAJOR MARINDIN.

Result :—WEST BROMWICH ALBION ... 2 goals.
PRESTON NORTH END ... 1 goal.

Preston North End, 1888-9

MILLS-ROBERTS	GRAHAM		HOLMES	RUSSELL		HOWARTH		DRUMMOND
	THOMPSON		DEWHURST	GOODALL	ROSS	GORDON		

PRESTON, who throughout the season had been steadily adding to their reputation, for the second year running found themselves at the Oval on this occasion to be matched with newcomers to the Finals in Wolverhampton Wanderers. Preston had previously put their last year's conquerors, West Bromwich Albion, out of the running, although only after an exceedingly close struggle.

The crowd of over 25,000 people, who had assembled at the Oval to witness this Final, were treated to one of the finest exhibitions of polished football ever seen. The passing of Preston North End was like clock-work, their defence on the few occasions it was called on, superb. In the first half, Dewhurst opened in scoring for Preston, Ross increasing the score shortly afterwards. With the change of ends the Wanderers were expected to show up much better, but they played a losing game from beginning to end, and when Thompson scored the third goal for Preston it was a fitting climax to a game in which the Wolverhampton eleven were outclassed in every department.

Preston created a remarkable record in this Final by going clean through the competition without having a goal scored against them, a feat which has only once been equalled since, namely, by Bury, in 1903. In this season they also won the championship of the newly-formed Football League without losing a match. The winning of the Cup and League in one season has only once since been equalled, namely, by Aston Villa, in 1897. The Preston North End players of these far-off days were perhaps the most wonderful club of all time, but it has to be borne in mind that Preston were the originators of open professionalism, and that no money was spared in assembling their famous players together. The team was chosen with marvellous precision and acumen, but it was the thoroughness of their training and their complete subordination of self to the interests of the side which made North End supreme.

Referee :—MAJOR MARINDIN.

Result :—PRESTON NORTH END ... 3 goals.
WOLVERHAMPTON WANDERERS Nil.

Blackburn Rovers, 1889-90

JAS. SOUTHWORTH   JOHN SOUTHWORTH   HORNE   DEWAR
LOFTHOUSE   CAMPBELL   FORBES   WALTON   TOWNLEY
BARTON   FORREST

THE prevailing cry before the match was "Any odds on Blackburn," an assurance that was to be amply justified by their record score, which, in fact, has only been equalled once since.

A great crowd, which severely taxed the available accommodation at the Oval, assembled to do honour to the presence of the Rovers, who, although they had been unable to survive to the Final in the three previous seasons, had established a firm reputation as born Cup-fighters.

The Rovers shaped like a winning eleven right from the kick-off, Wednesday being kept on the defensive practically from start to finish. Townley scored for the Rovers within six minutes of the start, three more goals following before half-time. Mumford headed the only goal for the Wednesday in a sudden break-away early in the second half, but during the remainder of the time they were kept penned in their own half. Lofthouse and Townley quickly put the Rovers further ahead, and but for the Herculean labour on the part of Morley and Bradshaw the score against Wednesday would have been even larger.

From the outset the men from Sheffield were hopelessly outplayed, diminutive full-back Morley alone playing his game, to such an outstanding degree indeed that he was carried shoulder-high off the field at the close of play. Sheffield, whose first appearance it was in the Final, had been anticipated to put up a much better fight, particularly as they had easily ousted Bolton Wanderers in the semi-final. It is questionable, however, if any team in England could have held the Rovers on the form they displayed in this game, and Townley established a record on his own by scoring three goals—two in the first and one in the second half. The total score of 6—1 stood as a record until 1903, when Bury slightly improved on it by carrying off the Cup with a score of 6—0.

Referee :—MAJOR MARINDIN.   *Result :*—BLACKBURN ROVERS   ...   6 goals.
                                               SHEFFIELD WEDNESDAY   ...   1 goal.

Blackburn Rovers, 1890-1

| BRANDON | | PENNINGTON | | BARTON | | SOUTHWORTH | | DEWAR | | FORREST |
| LOFTHOUSE | | WALTON | | FORBES | | HALL | | TOWNLEY | | |

THE Rovers, who had beaten Sheffield Wednesday in the previous season's Final by the record score of six goals to one, were thought to be up against a much stiffer proposition in tackling the players from Nottingham. Not that the county players were a brilliant lot, but after the form they had displayed in qualifying for their visit to the Oval, it was confidently anticipated that they had a rare chance of carrying off the coveted trophy. The Rovers, in the first half, were much smarter on the ball than their opponents, and thanks to goals scored by Dewar, Southworth and Townley, led 3—0 at half-time. This total was flattering to the Blackburn Rovers' eleven but hardly representative of the run of the play.

On the few occasions in this portion of the game when the County were attacking, they seemed quite unable to push home any advantage, and although possibly unlucky on one or two occasions, all their efforts seemed to be delivered in a somewhat faint-hearted fashion. In the second half, Notts gave promise of a much better performance, playing up gallantly and working the ball up in grand style. Again, however, their finishing efforts were of an extremely mild nature, and with the exception of a goal scored by Oswald, the fine play of the Rovers' backs frustrated every attempt to pierce their defence. The Rovers' defence was of a very safe character, the backs in particular being exceedingly accurate in their kicking. There was but little to choose between the forward lines—Hendry was outstandingly the best of the backs, and Calderhead the most prominent of the halves.

All through the game the Rovers displayed the better combination and greater resource, and this, to a great extent, was the means of enabling them to carry off the Cup for the fifth time.

Goal-nets and the penalty kick were introduced during this season.

Referee :—C. J. HUGHES.

Result :—BLACKBURN ROVERS ... 3 goals.
NOTTS COUNTY ... 1 goal.

West Bromwich Albion, 1891-2

BASSETT   REYNOLDS   READER   PERRY   GROVES   GEDDES
    NICHOLSON   MCLEOD   NICHOLLS   PEARSON   MCCULLOCH

THIS Final at the Oval goes down to history as the last of many thrilling encounters for the Cup played on this world-famous cricket ground.

It had been realised for some time by the authorities that the ever-increasing popularity of the Final necessitated the accommodation of a ground with a much greater holding capacity, and for the two years following the Final was played at Manchester and Everton respectively.

The Villa forwards, in the early portion of the game, gave every promise of sustaining their reputation for combination, but after play had been in progress for some time, the back line of the Albion had little difficulty in destroying what little combination was attempted. That the play of the Villa was disappointing is stating the matter mildly, as on several occasions they had opportunities to score, but seemed quite unable to send in a shot good enough to beat the Albion goalkeeper, Reader.

The Albion were superior in every department of the game, although with such a magnificent line of speedy forwards it was a matter of surprise that only Geddes and Nicholls succeeded in scoring in the first half.

Bassett was the hero of the day and undoubtedly the fastest runner on the field. In addition, he was the most unselfish of players, always keeping his proper position and centreing with unerring accuracy. He was an important factor in the placing of the ball on each occasion when the goals were scored in the first half, as well as when Reynolds scored the third and final goal of the match.

The Albion secured their victory by superior play and generalship. When playing against the wind they acted on the defensive, husbanding their resources and watching their opportunities. In their defence they were cool and collected, and it appeared as if they knew they were the better team.

Referee :—J. C. CLEGG.   *Result :*—WEST BROMWICH ALBION ... 3 goals.
                                       ASTON VILLA ... ... Nil.

Wolverhampton Wanderers, 1892-3

BAUGH   MALPASS   ALLEN   ROSE   KINSEY   SWIFT
TOPHAM   WYKES   BUTCHER   WOOD   GRIFFIN

THE ever-increasing crowds clamouring to see this tit-bit of the Association game had necessitated a change of venue from the London Oval, but even the spaces of Fallowfield, Manchester, were strained to breaking point to contain the 40,000 enthusiasts who assembled to see the game.

The attendance was a record one and many of the barricades were swept away by the swaying crowd—a wonderfully good-natured one, however—who, although encroaching on the touch line, but little interfered with the progress of the game.

The play displayed by both teams was far removed from what one was warranted to anticipate from the character of the elevens. Combination was singularly lacking on both sides, bouts of fantastic kicking being indulged in without the slightest attempt at placing or manipulating the ball.

Neither set of forwards ever got really settled down, possibly accounted for by the fact that the backs played such a determined tackling game. The back play on both sides was, in fact, really good, in distinct contrast to the balance of play, although both goalkeepers, Williams and Rose, were responsible for some brilliant saves.

The winning and only goal scored for the Wanderers in the second half by Topham from a most remarkable screw shot resulted in considerable controversy, and a protest was lodged by Everton with the referee. The score, however, after consideration by the Association, was allowed to stand.

The Wanderers fought a strenuous fight, and on the run of the play won a well-earned victory. In the first portion they did not have as much of the game as their opponents, but in the second half they rallied grandly and had hardly turned a hair at the end of the game, whereas Everton were tiring rapidly, and seemed to have trained right off colour.

Referee :—C. J. HUGHES.

Result :—WOLVERHAMPTON WANDERERS ... 1 goal.
EVERTON   ...   . Nil.

D

Notts County, 1893-4

BRAMLEY	HARPER	CALDERHEAD	TOONE	HENDRY	SHELTON
WATSON	DONNELLY		LOGAN	BRUCE	DAFT

A CROWD estimated at 32,000 assembled at the new venue at Everton which, in view of the vastly improved arrangements made for their comfort, compared somewhat unfavourably with the gathering at Manchester the previous year, as regards number of attendance.

The game was an extremely one-sided one and the merits of the play are hardly reflected in the score. Excitement ran high when Cassidy put the ball in motion, which was in no way lessened when it was seen that the County were determined on a dashing open game. Their combination was as perfect as one could wish, and the ball was kept moving at a rare pace. They took no liberties, but played as one man. Their knowledge of each other's play was amazingly perfect and in direct contrast to the wild efforts of the Wanderers. Logan was an outstanding performer, both in the first and the second halves, and greatly enhanced his already enviable reputation. He was an ideal centre, feeding both his wings most perfectly, while his shooting at goal was deadly accurate.

The Wanderers played all the science they knew, but were in sore straits to keep in check the resistless press of the County who, at half-time, were leading by 2 goals to nil. When they entered on the second half Bolton, for a brief space, looked like reversing the one-sided state of matters, but they had to reckon with an opposing force whose whole existence seemed staked on carrying the Cup to where the Trent flows. Two more goals fell to the wizardry of Logan, and although time after time the Wanderers tried to break through the County defence they were pulled up before the back-mark men were called into action. Almost on the call of time Bentley scored for the Wanderers, a very lucky goal, entirely through Toone slipping.

King Edward (then Prince of Wales) became patron of the Football Association this season.

Referee :—C. J. HUGHES.

Result :—NOTTS COUNTY	...	4 goals.
BOLTON WANDERERS	...	1 goal.

Aston Villa, 1894-5

REYNOLDS   SPENCER   DEVEY   WILKES   WELFORD
ATHERSMITH   CHATT   COWAN   RUSSELL HODGETTS   SMITH

BY scoring within a few seconds after the commencement of this Final, Chatt, for the Villa, had the satisfaction of not only registering the winning goal, but the distinction of being the first man to score in a Cup Final on the Palace ground, which in the years to come was to be the scene of many historical encounters. Nearly 45,000 people welcomed the return of the Final pageant to the Metropolis, and both elevens were impartially encouraged. The sun shone brilliantly in an almost cloudless sky, and the happy, contented nature of the attendance can be gauged on remembering that one bellman was sufficient to clear the playing field of spectators both at the commencement of the match and at half-time. The only goal of the match, scored by Chatt, was from a sensational bit of play, and decidedly lucky. Devey had started the ball in motion towards Reader's goal and Perry, in saving, kicked out. From the throw-in Chatt got possession and before anyone could realise the fact the Villans had scored, Chatt's shot reaching the net off Horton in such a manner that Reader had no earthly opportunity of saving. It was unfortunate that Horton misjudged the velocity of the shot, for as events proved, he was the innocent means of putting his side out of court in less than a minute from the start. The Albion did not take this misfortune lying down. The game was thoroughly well contested on both sides, the first half, in particular, being played at almost break-neck speed. The second half was pretty well a repetition of the first, the play fluctuating from end to end, but strive as they might the Albion could not draw level, Bassett in particular putting in some brilliant pieces of work. Both teams tired towards the finish, the marvel being that they had been able to keep up such a terrific pace for so long in the heat of a scorching sun. The Cup, while on exhibition at Birmingham, was stolen, and never afterwards recovered.

Referee :—J. LEWIS.   *Result :*—ASTON VILLA   ...   ...   1 goal.
                                                 WEST BROMWICH ALBION   ...   Nil.

Sheffield Wednesday, 1895-6

EARP		LANGLEY		BELL		SPIKESLEY
	BRANDON		MASSEY			PETRIE
CRAWSHAW		BRASH		BRADY		DAVIS

CLOSE on 50,000 spectators massed round the slopes of Sydenham where, for the second year in succession, the Association had decided to hold the Final for the Cup. Those present, who attended the previous year, were treated to a precisely similar exhibition of the tactics which won the Cup for the Villa, Spikesley, for Sheffield, scoring within one minute of the start. Unlike the goal scored by Chatt the previous year, where a certain amount of luck was attached, the same criticism could not be levelled against this performance. Before the vast concourse had properly realised that the game was actually in progress, a splendid combined run by Davis and Spikesley had resulted in the latter scoring. The Wolves, after this unexpected reverse, strenuously tried every move to get on level terms again, using their superior weight somewhat unmercifully, with the only result, however, that fouls were more frequent than goals. An equalising goal came in a very unexpected manner, as from a foul for hands Black sent the ball into the net. For a brief space after this bit of luck, the Wolves had slightly the better of the exchanges, but resorting to their old habit of long kicking and rushing, their efforts were easily thwarted. Spikesley then got busy on his own and put the Wednesday ahead with a terrific shot which hit the upright and went into the net. On the resumption, play fluctuated from end to end, both goals in turn escaping disaster. Towards the end of the game the Wolves had all the best of the play, but, despite their repeated attacks, do what they would they could not get over the Wednesday defence.

On the run of the day's play Sheffield Wednesday were just about value for their win, but with a little bit of luck the decision might easily have gone in the other direction. Lord Kinnaird, who had been a prominent exponent of the game and played in several Finals of the amateur days, had the privilege of presenting the new Cup and Medals to the players.

Referee :—CAPT. W. SIMPSON.

| *Result* :—SHEFFIELD WEDNESDAY | ... | 2 goals. |
| WOLVERHAMPTON WANDERERS | ... | 1 goal. |

Aston Villa, 1896 - 7

SPENCER   WHITEHOUSE   EVANS   CRABTREE
JAS. COWAN   ATHERSMITH CAMPBELL   DEVEY   WHELDON   JOHN COWAN   REYNOLDS

AN attendance of 65,000 clearly demonstrated the amazing interest taken in this annual struggle
for supremacy, this number beating the record for any football match then held for the England
versus Scotland game, which totalled 51,000. Magnificent weather again favoured the occasion,
and the ground at the Palace was in perfect playing condition. This was possibly one of the best Finals
played in the series of the competition. On both sides the football was good and no one could have
wished to see better half-back play than that of Reynolds, Cowan and Crabtree. The pace was hot throughout, yet the men were going as strongly at the finish as at the beginning.

Campbell, from a magnificent pass by Devey, opened the scoring for the Villa, Bell, for Everton,
shortly afterwards equalising. A few minutes later a free kick against Cowan gave Boyle his opportunity
of kicking the second goal for Everton. This lead did not last for long, as dashing away straight from the
kick-off Crabtree deftly placed the ball for Wheldon to equalise. Shortly afterwards Crabtree headed
the third and winning goal for Aston. Although led by 3 goals to 2 at half-time Everton had played a
remarkably sound game and there was really little to choose between the two teams. The second half
was also closely contested, but although strongly pressing towards the finish Everton could not pierce
the Villa defence. The Birmingham team deserved to win and the score is a true reflex of the value of the
play. Both sets of forwards had put up a sterling exhibition of high-class football, but as far as the winners
were concerned it was in their half-back line that their real strength lay and their superiority here gave
them the victory.

Aston Villa this season also won the League Championship, so equalling the record of Preston
North End who had completed the double in 1889.

Referee :—J. LEWIS.

Result :—ASTON VILLA   ...   ...   3 goals.
EVERTON   ...   ...   2 goals.

Nottingham Forest, 1897-8

FORMAN   RITCHIE   ALLSOP   McPHERSON   WRAGG   SCOTT
  McINNES   RICHARDS   BENBOW   CAPES   SPOUNCER

JOHN GOODALL, who played on the right wing for Derby County, very unselfishly summed up this game by his remark "the best team won." All the famous writers had predicted an easy victory for Derby, and credit must be extended to the Forest, not only for their fight against redoubtable opponents and also against popular sentiment. That the Forest, on the run of the day's play, were the best eleven every impartial critic cordially agreed, although the second goal scored, and which undoubtedly gave Notts the victory, was the outcome of an error of judgment on the part of the Derby custodian. It was a fitting tribute to his years of unswerving fidelity to the club of his adoption that Wragg should at last have been chosen to captain it when the "blue ribbon of the football world" was destined to come their way. An early sunshine had given way to a leaden-hued sky when the ball was set in motion before a crowd estimated at 70,000. Capes, from a free kick taken by Wragg, was the first to open the scoring. Roused by this reverse the County quickly got on the offensive and gave their only good showing of the match. They pressed determindedly, almost savagely. Still they were kept at bay and after their first onslaught had died away, Notts soon got busy again. Derby were the next to score, however—from a foul by Forman—the ball going into the net off Bloomer's cranium. Capes scored the next goal, putting Notts 2—1 ahead at half-time. The second half was nearly always in favour of Notts, although it was not until near the close that McPherson scored the third and final goal.

Forward Notts Forest were distinctly more in touch with each other than was the case in the opposition front line. Their chief merit was cohesion, although there were many striking examples of individual brillance. Their usual accurate construction gave way to defensive tactics towards the close, but their useful lead, no doubt, justified this cramping of the play.

Referee :—J. LEWIS.

Result :—NOTTS FOREST   ...   3 goals.
             DERBY COUNTY   ...   1 goal.

Sheffield United, 1898-9

HEDLEY   JOHNSON   BOYLE   FOULKE   ALMOND   MORREN
    BENNETT   BEERS   NEEDHAM   THICKETT   PRIEST

NOTHING appeals to the masses more than right-down dogged pluck, and the fact that the United had gone through the amazing experience of having to fight their semi-final against Notts Forest, the holders of the Cup, on four occasions on four different grounds, had established them as remarkable favourites with the majority of the 74,000 gate who witnessed the game. The interest that these sensational re-plays had aroused throughout the country was naturally unbounded, and it is questionable if ever a football eleven has been honoured with such universal well-wishing. Derby, who had been beaten by Notts Forest in the previous year's Final, were extremely confident of being able to annex the spoils of this match, and when, thanks to Boag, half-time was whistled, with the score standing 1—0 in their favour, their hopes looked like being realised. Sheffield, contrary to the hopes of the crowd, had by no means distinguished themselves during this period, but on the change of ends Sheffield held the mastery throughout, and it was in no uncertain way that this latter eventuality was accomplished. Shortly after the resumption of play Bennett equalised with a beautiful " header," and with Beers, Almond and Priest adding to their score, the United triumphantly carried off their first Cup. The team from Sheffield had given a really brilliant display during the last half hour and was a fitting culmination to a strenuous season's work, as they had met with more than ordinary difficulties in order to win their way through to the Final. The luck of the draw had been dead against them and in phenomenal favour of Derby who, however, had once again to taste the bitter pill of defeat.

The game was played at an unusually fast pace, but with the exception of a short period in the first half Derby County never looked like a winning eleven. It is questionable, indeed, if they would even have been able to score their solitary goal but for the assistance of a strong breeze.

Referee :—A. SCRAGGS.

Result :—SHEFFIELD UNITED   ..   4 goals.
           DERBY COUNTY   ...   1 goal.

Bury, 1899 - 1900

DARROCH   THOMPSON   DAVIDSON
PRAY   LEEMING   ROSS
RICHARDS   WOOD   McLUCKIE   SAGAR   PLANT

SOUTHAMPTON, the first professional Southern Club to survive a semi-final in the Cup—they were knocked out by Notts Forest, the ultimate winners in 1895, when the game was played in a blinding snowstorm—at last reached the goal of their ambition when they found themselves faced at the Crystal Palace by Bury.

The opening of the war in South Africa was the first time that the winter game had been interfered with by the " clash of arms," and many prominent players had departed for the front. Gates in these troublous days of disaster had naturally fallen off, but the enthusiasm for professional football which had blazed out with the Cup Competition, resulted in a remarkable attendance to witness this game.

Southampton, who had beaten Newcastle United, Everton, West Bromwich Albion and Reading in order to reach the Final were outstandingly the favourites with the crowd who saw visions of the coveted trophy returning to the South after a lapse of nearly 20 years. A tricky wind spoilt what would have been otherwise a perfect day and completely upset all opportunities of combination.

The Lancashire eleven were quick to grasp the changed conditions and abandoned their usual short passing game—tactics which soon resulted in McLuckie opening their score from a corner kick by Richards. McLuckie and Wood soon afterwards added to their total, half-time arriving with the score 3—0. The second half was practically a repetition of the first, and although only one further goal was scored—Plant from a corner kick—Bury ran out easy winners.

Southampton had a team of which they were justly proud, and player for player it could hardly be said, in point of reputation, that Bury were comparable, but, fit as the proverbial fiddle, grit and sheer doggedness cleared the Lancastrian path to triumph.

Referee :—A. G. KINGSCOTT.   *Result :*—BURY   ...   ...   4 goals.
SOUTHAMPTON ...   ...   Nil.

Tottenham Hotspur, 1900-1

CAMERON   ERENTZ   CLAWLEY   TAIT
   SMITH   MORRIS   HUGHES   JONES   KIRWAN
     BROWN   COPELAND

NEVER in the history of football had such interest been taken in a Final Cup Tie as marked this occasion at the Palace, when the hope of the South, the popular " Spurs," had qualified to meet Sheffield United, winners of the Cup two years previously. The scene presented one of the most magnificent spectacles possible on this splendid ground, where every available point of vantage was occupied by a crowd estimated at over 110,000 strong. The " Spurs " were tremendous favourites, although they were up against a very stiff proposition in the " Blades." Priest opened the scoring for Sheffield after about twenty minutes of exciting play. Brown headed an equalising goal shortly afterwards, half-time arriving with the score one all.

Brown put the " Spurs " ahead early in the second half, but not to be denied, Sheffield pressed strongly, and Bennett headed an equaliser. No further score resulting, the re-play was ordered to take place at Bolton.

After the enormous crowd which had witnessed the drawn game at the Palace, the attendance of about one-third the number was very disappointing. The men from Tottenham, contrary to anticipations, gave the United a fast and determined game, and although one under at half-time, they fairly rushed the Sheffield eleven off their feet in the second half, running up a sequence of three goals without giving their opponents a chance. Cameron, Smith and Brown were responsible for the scoring of these goals, and hard as Sheffield tried to reduce the lead, they found the Tottenham defence impregnable. So what was denied to Southampton the previous year, was given to the gallant " Spurs "—the first victory for a Southern Club in the Cup Final for twenty years. Tottenham had never previously reached the final stage for the Cup, and had their victory taken place in the Metropolis their reception baffles imagination.

Referee :—A. G. KINGSCOTT.

Result :—TOTTENHAM HOTSPUR   ...   3 goals.
          SHEFFIELD UNITED   ...   1 goal.

Sheffield United, 1901-2

JOHNSON   THICKETT   FOULKE   BOYLE   WILKINSON   NEEDHAM
BARNES   COMMON   HEDLEY   PRIEST   LIPSHAM

SOUTHAMPTON, who had made an unsuccessful debut in the Final three years previously, were tremendously popular favourites with the crowd, but the "Blades," who had drawn one game and just beaten in the re-play with the "Spurs" the previous year, were confidently expected to win. The terrible catastrophe at Ibrox Park at the England *versus* Scotland match undoubtedly affected the attendance, which was 40,000 down on that of the previous year. There was very little between the players in the first 40 minutes, the South holding their own in a very moderate exhibition. The players seemed to lack the dash which characterised the play in previous Finals. Everything was in favour of scoring, but the men did not seem to take advantage of their opportunities. At half-time there was no score. On the resumption, Common scored for Sheffield who looked like winning through, but three minutes before the call of time Harry Wood sensationally equalised for the "Saints."

The football on neither side could possibly be described as brilliant, but was consistent and interesting as an exhibition of two distinct styles of play.

The re-play, again staged at the Palace, failed to attract the interest of the previous Saturday's encounter. Play settled down to stern business immediately on the kick-off and showed vast improvement on the previous Saturday's drawn game. Within three minutes of the start Hedley smartly intercepted a pass from Lipsham and opened the scoring for Sheffield. The "Saints" pressed and were unlucky not to equalise before half-time, when the score stood 1—0. On the change of ends, Southampton forced the pace, and Brown, after a terrific rush, equalised from a corner kick by Chadwick. Barnes then scored a second goal for Sheffield, which proved the decider, and Sheffield carried home the trophy for the second time in their career. Barnes replaced Bennett in the re-play.

Referee :—T. KIRKHAM.

Result :—SHEFFIELD UNITED   ...   2 goals.
SOUTHAMPTON   ...   ...   1 goal.

Bury, 1902-3

RICHARDS   SAGAR   LEEMING   ROSS
THORPE   PLANT   MONTEITH
WOOD   LINDSAY   JOHNSTON   McEWAN

NEVER in the history of the Football Association Cup has any club suffered such a sweeping defeat as did Derby County in the presence of 63,000 spectators at the Palace on this occasion. The victory of Bury was hardly what one would call a complete surprise, in view of the amazing record of the team who had gone completely through the competition without having a single point scored against them. Bury were not a team of stars, but practical men who were as physically fit as possibly could be.

The first half of the game was fairly evenly contested, Ross, for Bury, being the only one successful in finding the net, and the play certainly gave no evidence of the holocaust to be witnessed during the later period.

In the second half Sagar scored within two minutes of the kick-off, and then Bury simply ran their opponents off their feet. Four more goals followed in rapid succession, Leeming, Wood and Plant registering points. Leeming then made a fine solo run and scored the final goal of the match with a beautiful shot. The last half-hour was entirely devoid of interest. It was an almost incredible result, for Derby County were a very fine team, and no one was prepared to see them so completely outplayed at all points of the game. By winning the cup without having a goal scored against them Bury equalled the record created by Preston North End (the " Invincibles ") in 1889, and while the game of football is ever fruitful in surprises it is doubtful if this record will ever be excelled.

The grit and the determination of the Bury eleven recalled the Final at the Palace three years previously when they administered a terrific drubbing to the hope of the South (Southampton) to the tune of 4—0. There was no fluke about that result, and there was emphatically none about this.

Referee :—J. ADAMS.   *Result :*—BURY   ...   ...   6 goals.
DERBY COUNTY   ...   ...   Nil.

Manchester City, 1903-4

BURGESS   FROST   GILLESPIE   McMAHON   HYNDS   HILLMAN   ASHWORTH
        LIVINGSTONE   MEREDITH   TURNBULL   BOOTH

ALTHOUGH from the point of view of Southern football this match did not rouse nearly so much interest as if a Southern team had been playing, the game was remarkable for the fact that two Lancashire clubs were meeting in the Final for the first time. The attendance of 61,000 was outstanding testimony to the ever-increasing fascination of the sport in the Metropolis. The general expectation was that Manchester would win, as they had been playing most consistently throughout the season, and both individually and as a side they were thought to be stronger, although the experience of Bolton in such matches was to their advantage. It is said that the Final Tie does not as a rule show the two teams at their best : the tension and excitement are apt to upset even the best balanced side. This, in some degree, was true as regards this Final, but although neither side gave a really great exhibition of football, the form shown was as a whole as good as the average. The City played the more scientific football, but as the game went on there was not much to choose between the rival elevens. It was an interesting match to watch from the fact that the result was in doubt up to the last minute. Bolton were not such a finished side as their opponents, but deserved every credit for the fine fight which they made. Meredith scored the only goal of the match 20 minutes from the start, but although Bolton played up pluckily they could not equalise. In the early part of the second half Bolton had much the better of the game and once or twice came near equalising. No further score was registered and the best of by no means two brilliant teams carried the Cup to Manchester.

As the Manchester City club had only been in existence for about ten years, their feat in carrying off the Cup on the first occasion they reached the Final was a performance of distinct merit, particularly as their opponents had played in the Cup Final as far back as the year when the " City " was founded.

Referee :—A. J. BARKER.   *Result :*—MANCHESTER CITY   ...   1 goal.
                                                BOLTON WANDERERS   ...   Nil.

Aston Villa, 1904 - 5

MILES   SPENCER   GEORGE
BRAWN   GARRATTY   HAMPTON   BACHE   HALL
PEARSON   LEAKE   WINDMILL

THE anticipation of seeing a titanic struggle between Newcastle, reported to be the most scientific team in the country, and the Villa, who had won the Cup three times previously, attracted a crowd of over 100,000 to the Palace. As a rule these matches have failed to furnish the true form of the teams engaged ; skill has given way to mediocrity and the cause is keenness and over-anxiety. But in this instance the game broke away from tradition. The Villa played a wonderful game ; their great pace was bewildering to their opponents and their whole play went with a splendid swing. The side had the reputation for casting to the winds all the nice theories of the game, and it was the adoption of these methods that upset the Newcastle plans and gave their defence no rest. Although Hampton scored for the Villa within three minutes of the opening, tension was never relaxed, and the way the Villa constantly landed the ball into the mouth of the Newcastle goal made it remarkable that the score should not have been larger at the interval.

On the resumption, the United bustled to their work and for a time threatened to equalise the scoring. Their half-backs particularly distinguished themselves and repeatedly sent the ball dangerously near the Aston goal, only, however, to have it promptly banged back again. Towards the close Hampton scored again for the Villa, but although the United made tremendous efforts, the Villa goal remained intact. It was a great tribute to the Villa that they should have so completely mastered such a fine team as their opponents. The best football was played in the first half, but the tremendous pace maintained was entirely to the liking of Aston Villa who fully merited their victory, which was secured as the result of the finest exhibition seen in any Final for many years past.

The first £1,000 transfer fee was paid this season.

Referee :—P. R. HARROWER.

Result :—ASTON VILLA ... ... 2 goals.
NEWCASTLE UNITED ... Nil.

Everton, 1905-6

MAKEPEACE   YOUNG   TAYLOR   SCOTT   BALMER
    SHARP   BOLTON ABBOTT   SETTLE CRELLEY HARDMAN

AFTER their magnificent struggle in the previous year's Final, Newcastle were confidently expected to carry off this year's trophy, although much was expected in the way of good football from two teams of such proved pace and ability. These great expectations were never realised ; the play was commonplace, if not uninteresting, and the only satisfaction about the match was that on the day's play the worse side lost. The players were trained to a minute, but seven months' wear and tear in League tournaments, while producing a state of nice fitness, had evidently deprived the players of their usual vivacity and " devil." With the exception possibly of Sharp, the teams played a disjointed, hard-kicking game, that possessed neither art nor efficacy. Neither side ever found a consistent swing for its game ; a good deal of the match was a mere kicking duel between the half- and full-backs. Luck did the rest and was mostly on the side of Everton. In the whole of the 90 minutes' play there were not a dozen hard shots.

Newcastle United in particular played a disappointing game, in no way approaching what one had been led to anticipate from their great reputation.

In the first half both goals in turn escaped spasmodic efforts to score, Sharp and Bolton being prominent for Everton, with Howie and Rutherford equally outstanding on the opposing side.

On the resumption, with the score sheet standing blank, there was really only one piece of concentrated judgment and execution, and this yielded the one goal of the match, which was scored by Young from a centre by Sharp, when the game had lasted an hour and a quarter.

The football was a mere lottery from beginning to end. The chances went mostly to Everton, but even Everton relied only on its one bit of real football to win. The form in the match was nothing like the form the sides had been capable of earlier in the season. Newcastle half-backs in normal conditions could not well be beaten for skill in controlling a game, but here they were all " at sea." The reason Everton won was that its players were more fortunate in their kicking and that Sharp showed great skill in trapping the ball and centreing.

Referee :—F. KIRKHAM.

Result :—EVERTON   ...   ...   1 goal.
           NEWCASTLE UNITED ...   Nil.

Sheffield Wednesday, 1906-7

BRADSHAW   BRITTLETON   LAYTON   LYALL   (Reserve)   (Reserve) BURTON BARTLETT
(Reserve) CHAPMAN   WILSON   CRAWSHAW STEWART   SIMPSON

THE long procession of beaten favourites in the Final had one more victim added to the score when the whistle sounded at the end of this game. A crowd of over 84,000 had assembled at the Palace and witnessed ninety minutes' of what may be fairly described as interesting, if not artistic football. It was generally understood that Everton were intrinsically the next best side to the leaders of the League, and, naturally, expected to win. The character of the football had much in common with that usually associated with Final ties ; neither side played quite as well as they were supposed to be capable of doing. There was much pace, the kicking was hard, the ball was much in the air, and fouls were plentiful. The Everton team included ten of the men who were successful in the previous Final, so that the ordeal of playing before a vast audience could not be urged as an excuse for the inability of Everton to find their real game. From the very first, however, they seemed embarrassed by the rushing and bustling tactics of the Wednesday. The play of Sheffield, if it did not often promise a score, kept the ball at the Everton end.

In the first half of the game, a mix-up on the part of the Everton backs enabled the first goal to be scored at the end of 20 minutes' play, Chapman swinging the ball into the mouth of Everton goal for Stewart to give it the final touch. During the closing minutes of the first half there was a glimpse of real football from the Everton side when the best goal of the match was scored by Sharp.

There was a general feeling that Everton would easily turn the game in the second half, but anticipations were not realised. From a throw-in about four minutes from the finish, the ball was hooked by Wilson across the mouth of the goal for Simpson, all unmarked, to quietly head it in the net.

This was one of the softest goals imaginable, but proved the deciding factor towards the defeat of Everton.

Referee :—N. WHITTAKER.

Result :—SHEFFIELD WEDNESDAY ... ... 2 goals.
EVERTON ... ... 1 goal.

Wolverhampton Wanderers, 1907-8

REV. K. HUNT   JONES   WOOLDRIDGE   LUNN   COLLINS   BISHOP
HARRISON   SHELTON   HEDLEY   RADFORD   PEDLEY

FOR the third time in four years Newcastle measured their strength for supremacy in the Final at the Palace. Judgment inclined to the United, whose skill, science and artistry were considered to be in an entirely different class to the Wanderers. But the all-English team of Wolverhampton sprung the usual Cup Final surprise. As the side enjoying the poorer prospects of victory, the Wanderers (a Second Division club) were popular favourites. The game was an extremely enjoyable one to watch ; it was always very fast and strenuous, full of incident and skilful football, and, best of all, fought out in the true sporting spirit with scarcely a suggestion of foul play or questionable tactics. The failure of Newcastle could be traced to the inability of their forwards to utilise some early chances of scoring, and to the gradual wearing down of the side by opponents who were rather the heavier and faster, and adept exponents of their own particular style of play. The " Wolves " never allowed their famous rivals, with their many internationals, Scotch, English and Irish, to find their short-passing combined game which had made them famous.

Hunt opened the score for the " Wolves " after half an hour's play, Hedley scoring a second goal three minutes later. The lead of two goals at half-time seemed sufficient to ensure success, until, following a corner, Veitch shot hard for Howie to turn the ball into the net.

Newcastle could make no further headway against a defence that never wavered, and in the last few minutes Harrison put the " Wolves " another goal ahead. The Newcastle men played well and only succumbed to superior strength. They had their opportunities, but were never left alone. Shots had to be taken with the utmost haste, no one ever getting clear away.

Newcastle were the classics ; Wolverhampton the workmen.

*Referee :—*T. P. CAMPBELL.   *Result :—*WOLVERHAMPTON WANDERERS   ...   3 goals.
NEWCASTLE UNITED   ...   ...   1 goal.

(Reserve) (Reserve)   MOGER   HAYES   BELL
MEREDITH DUCKWORTH   ROBERTS   J. TURNBULL   A. TURNBULL   STACEY
(Reserve)   (Reserve)   HALSE   WALL

COMPOSED of more experienced players, the majority of whose names had become famous, Manchester United gained the chief honours of the Association season deservedly. The play, which was extremely fast, with only an occasional sign of slackening, was marked by accuracy of kicking, strong tackling and, contrary to custom, heavy charging. Bristol City, in their desperate efforts to pull the match round, resorted to the old-fashioned vigour which, in recent years, has largely departed from the professional game, and in so doing gave opportunity for an exhibition of the amazing skill of Meredith and Wall, the Manchester wing forwards. Meredith, in particular, played beautiful football ; his clever forward work, rare control of the ball, sure passes and long shots into goal gave the deadliness to his side's attack. Had they kept the ball lower Manchester would probably have won with something to spare. Bristol, in the first half, showed their capacity to pass along the ground, and brought off some of the best combined runs seen during the afternoon. Lacking weight and the necessary pace they rarely got quite clear ; but, although their side had the worst of the play, they might have won had they shot better. Manchester United did most of the attacking, and the lead they gained in the first half remained with them to the end. Turnbull was the scorer of this goal, accomplished after Halse had hit the crossbar. The goal thus scored was the result of a serious misunderstanding on the part of two of the Bristol defenders, although there is no doubt that victory went to the side that deserved it on the run of the play.

Compared with the incisive deliberate methods of the United forwards, the efforts of the City front were ragged and disappointing. It was entirely owing to the cleverness of the Cottonopolis front rank that the score was turned in their favour.

Referee :—J. MASON.

Result :—MANCHESTER UNITED ... ... 1 goal.
BRISTOL CITY ... ... Nil.

Newcastle United, 1909-10

WILSON	MCCRACKEN	VEITCH	MCWILLIAM
CARR		LOW	LAWRENCE
HIGGINS	RUTHERFORD	SHEPHERD	HOWIE

FOR the fourth time in five years Newcastle made their appearance in the Final at the Palace, but once again they were denied the satisfaction of winning in the Metropolis. It cannot be said that the football yielded by this game was either scientific or artistic. Except during the last quarter of an hour—when the Newcastle men, the majority of whom possessed International Caps, played up to their reputation and sustained their attack in a clever and resourceful style—many faults were glaringly obvious. Partly because of the haphazard kicking of the half-backs, but chiefly because of their inability either to pass accurately or try a little dribbling, both sets of forwards were singularly ineffectual during the greater part of the game. Barnsley goal was the result of a fine inward pass and a clever shot by Tufnell, which glanced in off the post. The Newcastle eleven did very well in the closing stages of the match, their backs and half-backs keeping the ball down and feeding the forwards accurately. The equalising goal for Newcastle was headed in by Rutherford, the fastest and cleverest wing on the field.

On the re-play at Liverpool, the Newcastle men showed clearly that they were a splendid side, and in dribbling, passing and general tactics they out-played Barnsley completely. They displayed a remarkable control over the wet and slippery ball, while their pace never slackened. There was no score at half-time, but during the second period Rutherford and Howie were always prominent, although Shepherd, who was given more scope than on the previous Saturday, had the satisfaction of scoring both goals, the second one being from a penalty.

Thus in this re-play Newcastle achieved what they had failed to do in four appearances at the Palace. Carr replaced Whitson in the re-play.

Referee :—J. T. IBBOTSON. *Result :*—NEWCASTLE UNITED ... 2 goals.
BARNSLEY ... ... Nil.

Bradford City, 1910-11

| (Reserve) | TORRANCE CAMPBELL | O'ROURKE SPIERS LOGAN | MELLORS | McDONALD ROBINSON (Reserve) | DEVINE | TAYLOR | THOMPSON |

NEWCASTLE UNITED, who had beaten Barnsley for the Cup at Liverpool the previous year after a drawn game at the Palace, had the unique experience of again drawing before the Sydenham crowd. Their opponents on this occasion were making their first appearance in a Cup Final. Contrary to anticipations, the United did not have matters all their own way. A gusty wind interfered with their usual combination and the elusive ball baffled the footwork and distance judgment of this accomplished eleven. They had practically all the play in the first half, but only on rare occasions were even in measure of scoring distance. With the wind in their favour for the second half, they again utterly failed to realise the anticipations of their supporters. The game was played honestly and fairly to the last ounce by both teams, and yet it always fell short of the spectacular element one is accustomed to anticipate in a match of this importance.

The re-play at Manchester was a big improvement on the goalless draw at the Palace, but in winning this match Bradford must be regarded as particularly fortunate. The strong wind blowing was a spoiling factor in many promising movements, and the resolute, if unpolished, tactics of Bradford quite upset the plans of Newcastle, admittedly the most scientific team of the day. Scarcely ever did their forwards show a glimpse of the sound combined play for which they were famous. A very bad blunder by Lawrence resulted in O'Rourke scoring the only goal of the match for Bradford about a quarter of an hour from the start. Newcastle had many opportunities to score, but failed to take advantage.

Bradford City had the honour of being the first team to be presented with the new English Cup.

This is a much more imposing specimen of the silversmiths' art than the old Cup, and as it was made by a local firm, it was very appropriate that Bradford should be the first to win it.

Referee :—J. H. PEARSON.

Result :—BRADFORD CITY ... 1 goal.
NEWCASTLE UNITED ... Nil.

Barnsley, 1911-12

LEAVEY (Reserve) COOPER
GLENDINNING DOWNS TAYLOR UTLEY
BARTROP TUFNELL LILLYCROP TRAVERS BRATLEY
MOORE

FOR the third year in succession no definite result was reached in the Final Tie played at the Palace, and for the second year running no goals were scored by either side. There could be no two opinions as to the spirit and earnestness prompting the players in the rival elevens, but they were unable to provide those electric thrills for the spectators which are the very salt of football strife. Of a truth the game is lame and tame to the vast majority, no matter how skilfully it be played, unless it yields goals and a decisive ending. There was neither of these essentials.

West Bromwich did most of the pressing in the first half, but the Barnsley defence could not be penetrated. There was a brightening up all round in the second half which gave one the impression that the players had been afraid previously to let themselves thoroughly out, and with any luck at all either side should have scored.

In the re-play at Sheffield a great improvement in the pace and keenness could not escape notice, and from the energy displayed the teams were obviously more at home at Bramall Lane than in the larger arena at Sydenham. The balance of play in both halves of this game was slightly in favour of the Albion, who created the impression of being the superior side in tactics and execution, without being able, however, to pull out just that little bit extra which meant all the difference between victory and defeat. The Albion were, in fact, strongly attacking the moment before their defence broke down. There being no score on the whistle going, extra time was played, and it was almost with the last kick of a prolonged struggle that Tufnell from a sudden breakaway put the winning goal through for Barnsley.

A crowd estimated at 38,000 witnessed this re-play, which compared rather unfavourably with the gate of 55,000 which saw the previous goalless draw.

Referee :—J. R. SCHUMACHER.

Result :—BARNSLEY ... ... 1 goal.
WEST BROMWICH ALBION ... Nil.

Aston Villa, 1912-13

LYONS   WESTON   HARDY
BACHE   HALSE   HAMPTON   STEPHENSON
WALLACE   BARBER   HARROP   LEACH

ALL attendance records for the Final were broken. The Villa eleven, who were destined to win the Cup for the fifth time, were nearly as popular idols with the crowd of over 120,000 as if they were members of a Southern club. As things turned out, the game, though appreciably better than many of the Final Cup-ties of the last few years, was merely good in parts. It was fast and open at the beginning, but the promise of a brilliant start was not kept up—chiefly because the backs on either side soon took to high kicking, and were also anxious to dispose of the remotest possibility of danger by getting the ball away into touch. It was seldom, indeed, that either line of forwards justified their high reputation. There was little or none of the brilliant passing at top speed which had distinguished the Villa in previous victorious years. On both sides too much time was wasted in mere pattern-weaving, and when a concerted attack was delivered the obvious thing was always done at the critical moment. The head-to-head passing was at times uncannily clever ; yet one felt that in some cases a piece of straightforward dribbling would have been more effective. On the whole the best feature of the game was the superlative excellence of the defence on either side. However awkward the position the backs contrived to get the ball safely away. Hardy, the best goalkeeper England has had for a long time, gave a delightful exhibition.

There can be no doubt that Aston Villa was slightly the better team at all points of the game—even at half-back, where Sunderland were supposed to have a distinct advantage. The more popular team ought certainly to have scored more than the single goal adroitly headed by Barber late in the second half, which Butler, the Sunderland goalkeeper, had no possible chance of saving. This winning goal was the outcome of a corner kick taken by Wallace and beautifully centred.

Referee :—A. ADAMS.   *Result :*—ASTON VILLA   ...   1 goal.
                                                  SUNDERLAND   ...   Nil.

Burnley, 1913-14

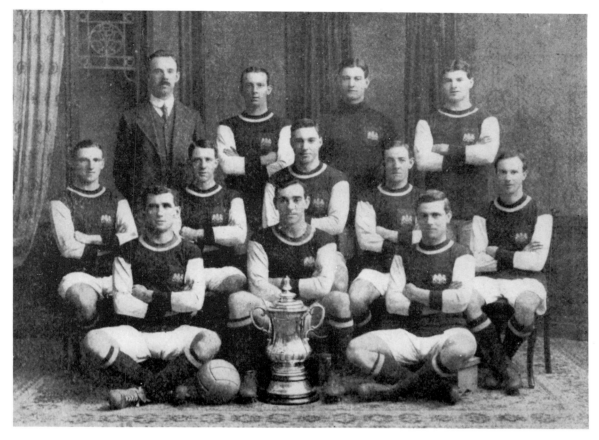

FREEMAN   HALLEY   LINDLEY   BAMFORD   HODGSON   BOYLE   SEWELL   NESBITT   WATSON   TAYLOR   MOSSCROP

FOR the first time in the history of the Cup, His Majesty King George attended and honoured the winners and runners-up by presenting the Cup and Medals. Widely diverse opinions were expressed on the merits of this Final played between two teams occupying a lowly position in the League. When the players settled down, Liverpool looked the better side ; the combination among their forwards was at times distinctly good. The Burnley forwards were too small to trouble the Liverpool defence seriously ; they forced corners, but were bundled off the ball unceremoniously whenever they tried to work into a position to shoot. When half-time came there had not been a single example of the sustained attacks which are so often seen in League football. Each team kept wrecking the other's combination, and it seemed highly probable that some brilliant bit of opportunism would determine the result of a guerilla game. Lacey and Freeman were obviously the outstanding players of genius taking part in the match, and, what is more, the only men who were not afraid of taking the responsibility of an unorthodox venture. For some minutes after the resumption the game was still desultory and disjointed. Then came Burnley's well-earned goal. Ten minutes of the second half had gone when Freeman got the ball and crashed it into the net with one of the most powerful shots one could wish to see. The Liverpool goalkeeper had no earthly chance of stopping this really fine shot. During the half hour following Burnley's goal the game certainly improved and the spectators were treated to thrilling movements on several occasions.

Grim earnestness and intense determination characterised the movements of both teams, but it is just possible that the one goal scored correctly reflects the respective merits of the play.

72,000 spectators attended and accorded H.M. The King a remarkable reception.

Referee :—H. S. BAMLETT.

Result :—BURNLEY ... 1 goal.
LIVERPOOL ... Nil.

Sheffield United, 1914-15

	ENGLISH		GOUGH		BRELSFORD		STURGESS	
COOK		FAZACKERLEY		UTLEY		MASTERMAN		EVANS
SIMMONS								KITCHEN

" You have played with one another and against one another for the Cup ; play with one another for England now."

THUS spoke the Earl of Derby when presenting the Cup and commending the spirit in which this Final had been played. The game took place at Manchester in a murky gloom quite in keeping with the surroundings associated with the second year of the World War. The usual exuberant spirits exhibited at all Cup Finals were depressingly absent ; no attempt to make it an excuse for a picnic was even attempted. The enthusiasm of even the man with the football fever fast upon him was replaced with a new psychology—it was a chastened unostentatious crowd. Chelsea played fairly well in the first half, but as the game progressed it was clearly demonstrated that neither in skill nor determination were they on the same plane as their more experienced opponents. Chelsea, in a degree most marked, utterly failed to reproduce that method and decisiveness of which they were admittedly capable. They were seldom as dangerous as the Sheffield men, who, caring less for the niceties of the game and having as their central idea the making of headway, were infinitely the better workmen. A misunderstanding between Molyneaux, the Chelsea goalkeeper, and his backs, allowed Simmons to open the scoring for the United ; a very soft goal, got more by fortune than design. On the change of ends, Sheffield were again the better side. Fazackerley secured their second goal, and Kitchen crowned the best individual effort of the day by getting a third.

Little did the public realise that five years of grim tragedy would elapse before another Final would be played, and statistics will never chronicle how many of those who heard and answered the call of Lord Derby saw their final Final.

Referee :—H. H. TAYLOR.

Result :—SHEFFIELD UNITED ... 3 goals.
CHELSEA ... ... Nil.

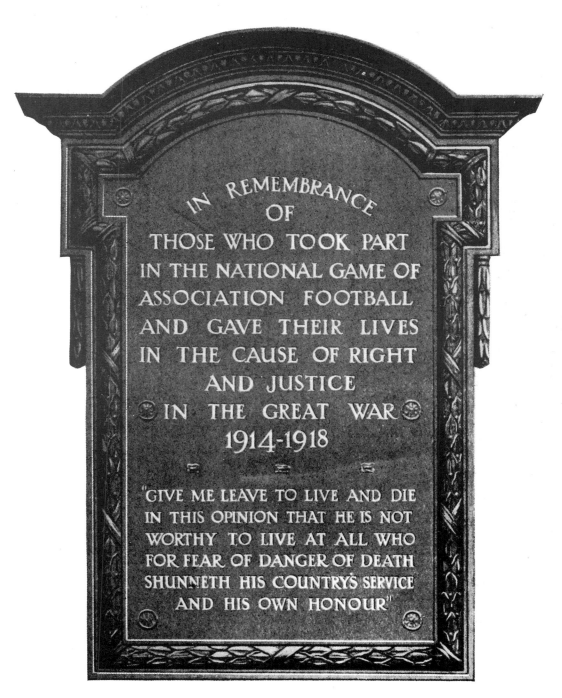

IN REMEMBRANCE
OF
THOSE WHO TOOK PART
IN THE NATIONAL GAME OF
ASSOCIATION FOOTBALL
AND GAVE THEIR LIVES
IN THE CAUSE OF RIGHT
AND JUSTICE
IN THE GREAT WAR
1914-1918

"GIVE ME LEAVE TO LIVE AND DIE
IN THIS OPINION THAT HE IS NOT
WORTHY TO LIVE AT ALL WHO
FOR FEAR OF DANGER OF DEATH
SHUNNETH HIS COUNTRY'S SERVICE
AND HIS OWN HONOUR"

"THEY PLAYED THE GAME"

Aston Villa, 1919-20

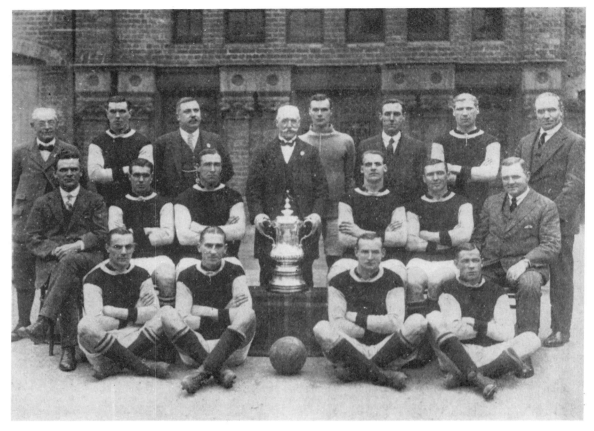

		SMART			HARDY			MOSS	
KIRTON			DUCAT			WALKER		STEPHENSON	
WALLACE			BARSON				WESTON		DORRELL

A GOOD-NATURED, good-tempered crowd of 50,000 souls assembled at Stamford Bridge to witness the first Final Tie of the English Cup to be played for since 1915. Aston Villa took the field with their tremendous cup-winning reputation behind them, but Huddersfield were a stout-hearted lot, full of confidence in themselves. The game was fast and strenuous, and there were several exciting incidents, but the absence of individual effort—except on the rarest occasions—was the most lasting impression of the game. Aston Villa from the very beginning were obviously the cooler players, but they were over-anxious to keep the ball moving from player to player, not always with the clearest motive. This perpetual swinging and hooking and heading the ball from one player to another set up the pace that kills—it tired Huddersfield out, who were not so ruthlessly efficient, more than it did Aston Villa—but there was also so much mechanical interception that nothing much seemed to come of it all. In the second half the teams themselves seemed to realise the fact and there were several clever dribbling runs by players who previously had seemed past praying for. Huddersfield played a sound defensive game which counteracted all the best-laid schemes of the Villa, who were unable to register any score during the first two halves. For the first time in the past half-century extra time was ordered to be played, and within seven minutes—although most people had given up all hopes of a definite result—Aston Villa suddenly forced a corner. The kick sent the ball skimming over the heads of the usual cluster of players in the goalmouth straight to the head of Kirton who just nodded it into the net, slightly diverted, so it was said, by the head of Wilson. Late chances that came the way of Huddersfield to equalise were missed, so Aston Villa for the sixth time carried off the coveted trophy.

Luck was in favour of the Birmingham men on this occasion.

Referee :—J. T. HOWCROFT.

Result :—ASTON VILLA ... 1 goal.
HUDDERSFIELD ... Nil.

Tottenham Hotspur, 1920-1

		CLAY	SMITH		WALTERS		McDONALD
BANKS	SEED	GRIMSDELL		HUNTER	CANTRELL	BLISS	DIMMOCK

THE " Spurs " did what was expected of them in winning the Cup in the presence of H.M. The King and an attendance of 72,000, who paid upwards of £13,000 in gate money, then easily a record for any football match. It was an interesting Final, the play being much better than usual, and although the " Spurs " won much more easily than is suggested by the score of a goal to nil, they did not have matters all their own way. The Wanderers put up a stubborn fight and a game defence, and saved all attempts to score against them in the first half. The winning goal came after about 10 minutes' play in the second half. It was a pass across field by Seed—a very favourite piece of Tottenham tactics—that gave Dimmock his chance. The ball was just diverted by Bliss's head, and then Dimmock once again defied criticism and tried to dribble his own way towards the Wolverhampton goal. He only half-beat Woodward and the crowd groaned in anguish. But Dimmock recovered his poise as quick as lightning, and, before either Woodward or the crowd could realise it, a terrific low shot had whizzed into the far corner of the net. Before the cheering had died down Tottenham were attacking again furiously, but by a supreme effort Wolverhampton repulsed all onslaught. Later Brooks had a great opportunity right in front of the " Spurs' " goal, but taking too long to steady himself had what looked like a certain goal charged down by Walters. Brooks was just a fraction too late—but a memorable fraction that might easily have changed the story of the second Final won by Tottenham.

Both goals had their escapes after this, but Tottenham maintained their lead, and had the distinction of bringing back the Cup to the South after a lapse of twenty years, thus repeating in a remarkable manner their performance of twenty years previously.

This was the second of three Finals played at Stamford Bridge.

Referee :—J. DAVIES.   *Result :*—TOTTENHAM HOTSPUR ... ... 1 goal.

WOLVERHAMPTON WANDERERS ... Nil.

Huddersfield Town, 1921-2

WOOD   SLADE   MUTCH   WILSON   WATSON   WADSWORTH
RICHARDSON   MANN   ISLIP   STEPHENSON   SMITH

THERE can be no more romantic story in the annals of football than the rise from obscurity to world fame of Huddersfield Town. Bankrupt shortly after the war, they were harassed by all kinds of financial complications. Notwithstanding those handicaps, the club managed to run into wonderful form, to such an extent that their exploits gripped the imagination of the public who rallied to their support, with the ultimate result that their monetary position was eased and the club put on a sound footing. Huddersfield had not long to wait consolation for their defeat in the Final two years previously, when they were only just beaten by the only goal scored after extra time had been played. The welcome return to the limelight of fame by Preston North End, was unfortunately marred, not only by an unsatisfactory defeat, but also by a most disagreeable and unworthy game. It was a disappointing exhibition, with neither side able to produce the football of which they were capable. There were many fouls, the majority of a technical kind, but the one that led up to the only goal was deliberate and cost Preston North End the game. No scoring took place in a very uninteresting first half, and twenty minutes had elapsed of the second half when Smith was obviously tripped up. He took the awarded penalty kick and drove in a hard low shot which found the net. The foul was a flagrant and typical one ; each side seemed equally determined to stop any player who looked dangerous, regardless of all ules written and unwritten.

Huddersfield thoroughly deserved to win, and to carry off the Cup was a well-merited climax to eleven years of strenuous endeavour and marvellous performance. They had gained promotion from the Second to First Division, created a record by winning the League Championship in three successive years, and have played in the Final on four occasions.

Referee :—J. W. D. FOWLER.   *Result :*—HUDDERSFIELD TOWN   ...   1 goal.
                                               PRESTON NORTH END   ...   Nil.

Bolton Wanderers, 1922-3

NUTTALL   HOWARTH   SEDDON   PYM   JENNINGS   ROWLEY (Reserve)
BUTLER   JACK   J. R. SMITH   JOE SMITH   VIZARD   FINNEY

THIS was the first Cup Final to be played at the Wembley Stadium, and was unquestionably the most unsatisfactory match ever decided in the history of the competition. The arrangements for shepherding the attendance were hopelessly inadequate ; 120,000 people passed the turnstiles and certainly another 100,000 rushed the barriers. This enormous and entirely unexpected concourse of spectators was possibly attracted by two reasons, firstly, to see how the plucky southern eleven would fare in the Final, and, secondly, to see the wonders of the much-lauded Stadium. When a quarter of a million people attempted to fit themselves into a space that was only designed to hold half this number it is really remarkable that nothing more serious than the encroachment on the playing pitch took place. The amazing patience and good humour of the police (not forgetting the genius on the ever-to-be-remembered white horse) and the adaptability of the public themselves saved the situation. Under the conditions which prevailed, however, it would be absurd to accept the result of this Final as indicative of the merits of the respective teams. The crowd were encroaching on the field when Jack opened the scoring for Bolton within two minutes of the start. Watson, three minutes later, failed to equalise with the Bolton goal yawning only a few yards in front of him. In the second half Smith kicked a somewhat remarkable goal for the Wanderers which, although it went into the net, bounced out again, but was allowed as a goal by the referee.

The disturbing conditions all around had keyed the players on both sides up to such a high point of tension, that as a match the play was disappointing. The only justification for the decision being allowed to stand as official was that the conditions were the same for both sides.

Bolton Wanderers on the day's play were a shade the better side.

Referee :—D. H. ASSON.

Result :—BOLTON WANDERERS   ...   2 goals.
WEST HAM UNITED   ...   Nil.

Newcastle United, 1923-4

LOW   COWAN   HARRIS   SPENCER   HAMPSON   HUDSPETH   MOONEY   GIBSON   McDONALD   SEYMOUR

BRADLEY   (Reserve)

PROFITING by the alarming experience of the previous year, much more adequate arrangements had been made at the Stadium for the comfort and safety of the attendance, although nothing approaching the numbers who had handicapped the play of the last Final ventured within the precincts of Wembley.

The most fervid supporters of the Aston Villa eleven could not disagree with the opinion that on the afternoon's play the better team won. The Villa were strong favourites before the commencement of the match, but Newcastle proved the better team if only because they conserved their energies sufficiently to enable them to come with an irresistible burst in the concluding stages. All through the first half, and the early portion of the second, Newcastle played second fiddle to the Villa, but in a thrilling last five minutes, when extra time seemed certain to be played, they twice pierced the Aston defence. The rain had made the ground greasy and treacherous, but considering the conditions the game was really good to watch: fast, keen and clean. Eight minutes before the finish Newcastle scored their first point: a brilliant piece of play. Spencer started a movement which enabled Harris to put in a tremendous and unexpected shot and finish off a perfect sample of combination. A minute later Aston Villa had the opportunity of equalising, but their effort was spoilt. The game had hardly been restarted when Seymour scored his spectacular goal. The ball had been sent out to him, a long, low pass, which he collected at full speed and before Jackson could quite realise what had happened, the ball was crashed into the right-hand corner of the net. Two goals in three minutes! Newcastle thoroughly deserved to win. Their first goal was the outcome of dash and understanding, their second the fruits of individualism and independence.

The glamour which surrounds the Aston Villa eleven possibly more than any other club when it comes to a Cup Final suffered a severe and unexpected set back, but their famous defence, strong as it had always shown itself in numerous displays, was thoroughly bewildered after Harris had broken through their defence and Newcastle took very good care to give them no opportunity of recovering.

Referee :—W. E. RUSSELL.

Result :—NEWCASTLE UNITED   ...   2 goals.

ASTON VILLA   ...   Nil.

Sheffield United, 1924-5

PANTLING	KING		COOK	SUTCLIFFE		MILTON		GREEN
	BOYLE			JOHNSON		GILLESPIE		
	MERCER					TUNSTALL		

AN item of especial interest with regard to this Final was the fact that it marked the first occasion that a Welsh team had ever taken part in one. Cardiff City had made a meteoric advance during their few years in first-class football, and this remarkable crowning to their achievements had stirred the hearts of their fellow countrymen to a degree that had to be seen to be realised. It is questionable if ever such a crowd of Welshmen had invaded London before. Literally tens of thousands, many of whom had no earthly chance of seeing the match, came to give heart to the team from Cardiff, and needless to say their popular national vegetable, the leek, was everywhere in evidence.

Sheffield United won on their merits. Cardiff never reached the level of skill one was accustomed to see in their League games. They played as if conscious of their inferiority, and yet their defence was as sound as the United's attack was strategic. It was always an exciting match, as indeed it was bound to be, but apart from spasmodic interludes the football was never first-class. Fourteen minutes before the interval the issue at stake was settled when Wake's hesitation gave Tunstall the opportunity to give the finishing touch to a long swinging pass from Pantling by dribbling to within a few yards from goal and pushing, rather than shooting, the ball into the Cardiff net. Sheffield deserved their victory, for they made the most of their one real chance. Cardiff really could not grumble at the result, for in the second half they had a remarkably easy chance to equalise, when any one of three practically unhampered forwards had the United goal at their mercy, but each in turn failed to make history. Gillespie, the Sheffield Captain, played a memorable game on this occasion, and his performance will long live in the recollection of those who were privileged to see it.

91,000 attended this Final.

*Referee :—*G. N. WATSON.

*Result :—*SHEFFIELD UNITED ... 1 goal.
CARDIFF CITY ... ... Nil.

Bolton Wanderers, 1925-6

HAWORTH　　NUTTALL　　PYM　　JENNINGS　　GREENHALGH
BUTLER　　　JACK　　J. R. SMITH　　JOE SMITH　　VIZARD　　SEDDON

F OR the second time in four years Bolton Wanderers won the Cup at Wembley Stadium, where, as in the previous season, admission could only be obtained by ticket. Despite the fact that the finalists were both Lancashire teams, over 91,000 passed the turnstiles. There have been many more exciting Finals, but few indeed that have been played so cleanly and fairly right from start to finish. The game was closely and vigorously contested, but it was twelve minutes to the finish when Jack scored the only goal of the match for Bolton.

The first half of the game was played at a fast pace throughout, and at times was distinctly interesting, the balance of the play being largely in favour of the Wanderers. It must be said, however, that although they had nearly all of the game they did not profit by it and many openings were wasted.

With the exception of the first few minutes in the second half, when Manchester City had a distinct opportunity of opening the scoring, the Wanderers again practically monopolised the remaining portions of the play.

From a pass by Vizard, who played beautifully throughout, Jack scored the winning goal, and although Manchester City made desperate efforts in the few remaining minutes to equalise—and nearly succeeded in doing so—Pym, the Wanderer's goalkeeper, who had already achieved some wonderful saves, proved his reliability and kept his goal intact. Manchester City played clever football, but it requires football of a more robust nature to win a Cup Final.

The receipts at this Final realised over £23,000. H.M. The King attended and presented the Cup and Medals at the conclusion.

Referee :—I. BAKER

Result :—BOLTON WANDERERS　...　1 goal.
MANCHESTER CITY　...　Nil.

Cardiff City, 1926-7

NELSON FARQUHARSON WATSON McLACHLAN
SLOAN IRVING KEENOR HARDY DAVIES
CURTIS FERGUSON

A NEW chapter in the history of the Association Cup was written as the result of this Final, when for the first time since its foundation it was won by a Welsh club—the first and only time the Cup had been taken out of England. Cardiff had given evidence of their remarkable progress by qualifying for the Final two years previously when they met with a narrow defeat at the hands of Sheffield United by the only goal scored. Cardiff put up a fine clean game, but it has to be admitted that their entry into the charmed circle of Cup winners was the result of a tragic error by the Arsenal goalkeeper. An additional irony could be found in the fact that Lewis was a Welsh International player.

The Arsenal, captained by a great player and personality in Buchan, had most of the game in the first half, but nerves and a lively ball helped to make most of the opening moves look exceptionally slow and futile. Repeated free kicks for off-side or foul tackles further broke up any sequence of movement. Any attacks by Cardiff may fairly be described as break-aways, as their forwards showed little or no signs of concerted combination. There was no score in the first half.

The Arsenal again showed to advantage in the opening exchanges of the second half, Buchan in particular distinguishing himself with short spells of brilliant dribbling and placing of the ball. The veteran Hardy, with his bald head and sturdy figure, was also always prominent. Twenty-five minutes' play of the second half had fluctuated from end to end when the tragic blunder dashed the aspirations of the Arsenal. The decisive movement started from a throw-in. Ferguson took a pass and drove a hard low shot at goal. Lewis appeared to field it brilliantly, but the ball seemed to twist on his chest and in grabbing it he sent it trickling over his own goal-line. An almost incredible trifle, but sufficient to enable Cardiff to take the Cup to Wales for the first time in the long history of the competition.

Referee :—W. F. BUNNELL.

Result :—CARDIFF ... 1 goal.
ARSENAL ... Nil.

Blackburn Rovers, 1927-8

RANKIN (Reserve) HUTTON CRAWFORD CAMPBELL JONES (Reserve)
THORNEWELL PUDDEFOOT ROSCAMP HEALLESS McLEAN RIGBY (Reserve)

IT was stated by the Wembley authorities that nearly one million applications for tickets had been received, but only 92,000 were privileged to see the game. Huddersfield were strong favourites, but Blackburn Rovers made fresh football history. The long space of 37 years had passed since that wonderful period of the competition when in nine Finals they had carried off the Cup on five occasions.

Huddersfield, a team of all the talents, disappointed miserably, so adding to the long list of beaten "certainties," whose skill as measured in League football failed hopelessly when it came to the final test—the Cup Final test. The downfall of Huddersfield began in the opening minute and in sensational fashion, when their goalkeeper allowed himself to be charged, ball in hand, almost into the net of his own goal. Roscamp shot the goal, following up with a fair and square change. This first score was undoubtedly somewhat lucky, but the other two, one scored by McLean in the first half and the other by Roscamp six minutes from the finish, were the result of clever play. The remarkable thing about the Rovers' victory was the confident and convincing way in which their rather derided forward line set about their particular tasks. They "took the wind out of their opponents' sails" in the first half by adopting strong forceful tactics, with the happy result that they led 2—0 at half-time.

In the early stages of the second portion of the game Rovers changed their plan of campaign and started packing their goal and kicking out. Huddersfield then promptly got into their stride and looked like showing their true form. Blackburn were quick to realise their mistake and although Jackson from a beautifully placed forward pass scored a somewhat remarkable goal for Huddersfield, the resumed dashing attacks by the Blackburn forwards resulted in Roscamp scoring the third goal.

Her Majesty The Queen, who accompanied the King, displayed great interest in the varying phases of the game.

Referee :—T. G. BRYAN. *Result :*—BLACKBURN ROVERS ... 3 goals.
HUDDERSFIELD TOWN ... 1 goal.

Bolton Wanderers, 1928-9

KEAN   HAWORTH   PYM   FINNEY   NUTTALL

BUTLER   McCLELLAND   SEDDON   BLACKMORE   GIBSON   COOK

BY beating Portsmouth, the ambitious but forlorn hope of the South, Bolton Wanderers created somewhat of a minor record, as having won the Cup in 1923 and 1926, this made their third victory, all scored at the Wembley arena. This consistent Cup fighting form had naturally weaned the balance of public opinion in their favour, but the men from Portsmouth had many sympathisers and supporters. The prettiest if not the most effective football of the day was exhibited by the losers, some of their passing and dribbling being particularly pleasing.

In the first half Portsmouth did most of the pressing and for a time hopes were revived that the Cup for another brief season was going to find a resting place in the South. If only a little more weight and determination had been added to their style and finesse, from the opportunities which came their way they might well have scored the first and generally decisive goal. During this period, contrary to anticipations, Bolton did not attempt to force the pace. They appeared to be playing so well within themselves, and were so much the more solid team both in weight and method, that in the exhausting atmosphere of a Cup Final they always promised to last longer than their more energetic opponents. The presence of six men in the Bolton team who had had previous experience of Wembley requirements helped to explain what were obviously considered and carefully thought out tactics.

The second half witnessed play of a much more robust and promising character, and although Bolton were unable to open their score until twelve minutes from the finish, they had the game well in hand all through this portion. Butler scored the first goal with a terrific shot which completely beat Gilfillan, and almost immediately afterwards a second goal was scored by Blackmore. This player proved as much a cause of Portsmouth's downfall as anyone.

Referee :—A. JOSEPHS.

Result :—BOLTON WANDERERS ... 2 goals.
PORTSMOUTH ... ... Nil.

Arsenal, 1929-30

BAKER   LAMBERT   PREEDY   SEDDON   HAPGOOD   JOHN
MR. H. CHAPMAN   JACK   PARKER   JAMES   T. WHITTAKER
HULME   BASTIN

HAVING drawn with their opponents in the League engagement at Huddersfield the previous Saturday, hopes ran high among the Arsenal admirers that they would succeed in bringing back the Cup to the Metropolis after a lapse of nine years and for the third time only in 48 years. In this expectation their supporters in the crowd of over 92,000 who attended were not disappointed, but they must have passed through many harrowing moments of anxiety and suspense before their anticipations were realised. This was no runaway victory for the Southern eleven, and particularly during the second half they were frequently hard put to it to keep the ball out of their goal; in fact, it was amazing that the almost continuous bombardment of Arsenal goal did not result in a score. Preedy, their goal-keeper, cleared with great brilliance and daring, but at times took risks which hardly deserved to succeed as they did.

In the first half Arsenal were distinctly the superior side. They opened with a dash and determination which was early rewarded by a goal scored by James, to whose skill and bold tactics most of the credit for this victory must be accorded. The scoring of an early goal in any Cup Final means much and is all important. In view of the hammering Arsenal defence had to go through in the second half, in this instance, it undoubtedly won the match. Huddersfield attacked strongly after this reverse and did everything that a team could do—except score an equaliser.

In the second half Huddersfield pressed almost continuously; Smith, their veteran star performer, accomplished wonders all the time. Repeatedly a goal seemed to be imminent, and just as regularly something cropped up to prevent a score. Then from an opportune kick by James, Lambert took a long lonely dash down the field, tricked Turner who came out to meet him, and scored the second goal.

Referee :—T. CREW.   *Result :*—ARSENAL ... ... 2 goals.
                                      HUDDERSFIELD ... Nil.

West Bromwich Albion, 1930-31

		PEARSON				
W. RICHARDSON	EDWARDS	GLIDDEN		MAGEE	CARTER	WOOD
	TRENTHAM	W. G. RICHARDSON		SANDFORD	SHAW	

A NOTEWORTHY performance was achieved by the Albion on this occasion when they not only placed the Cup for the third time to their credit, but also won promotion from the Second Division to the First Division—a feat never previously accomplished. This remarkable consistency was the reward of youthful enthusiasm and confidence. They played with absolute trust in one another and seemed instinctively to know when to do a thing and when to leave it to a partner. Richardson, in particular, was a perfect inspiration. Speedy, but unselfish, he was an outstanding example to his forwards who were infinitely superior to their opponents. The Birmingham forwards did not exhibit their usual standard of play—they did not appear to have the same good understanding as the Albion.

In contradistinction to the usual sunny weather one is accustomed to at Cup Finals, the first half opened with the rain falling down unmercifully, but, notwithstanding the unsatisfactory condition of the elements, the spectators were rewarded for their endurance by as spectacular a match as one could wish to see. Both sides were slow to get into their stride, but once the Albion did get going they were rarely far away from the Birmingham goal and they were good value for the point by which they led at half-time, scored by Richardson.

On the resumption, West Bromwich made the pace with a terrific and sustained attack, and but for some remarkable saves by Hibbs, the Birmingham goalkeeper, the margin of goals in favour of the winners would have been very much larger. Birmingham's solace for surviving this ordeal came in a goal scored by Bradford, but they had hardly finished congratulating themselves when a speedy combined rush by the Albion led to Richardson scoring the second and, as it proved, winning goal. The Albion well deserved their victory, and but for a sterling defence their score would have been larger.

Referee :—A. H. KINGSCOTT.   *Result :*—WEST BROMWICH ALBION ... 2 goals.
BIRMINGHAM ... ... 1 goal.

Newcastle United, 1931-32

	NELSON	MCINROY	FAIRHURST	
	MCKENZIE	DAVIDSON	WEAVER	
BOYD	MCMENEMY	ALLEN	RICHARDSON	LANG

A GAME that will be long remembered as that of the disputed goal. How far this decision affected the *morale* of the Arsenal and their subsequent play, no man will ever be able to tell.

An ideal day, a perfect playing pitch with two teams of almost equal merit, gave promise of a battle of the Trojans—and the public were not disappointed. Right from the kick-off to the call of time, thrill was added to thrill—tension was sustained almost to breaking point, and beyond question one of the fastest and cleanest exhibitions of first-class football ever witnessed was put up for the entertainment of the ninety-odd thousand spectators who were privileged to be present.

There was no weak spot on either side, there was outstanding brilliance on both. The opening goal for the Arsenal was scored by Jack from a masterly pass by Hulme who, only a few days previously, was an extremely doubtful player. It looked for a time as if history would repeat itself—that the team who scores the first goal wins the Cup. It was not to be, however, and when Richardson, from an admittedly doubtful position, hooked the ball across for Allen to equalise for Newcastle it was sensed that a fight was in store. The honours in the first half were fairly divided, but the same cannot truthfully be said of the second. Newcastle right through this period were a winning eleven. The Arsenal defence was magnificent, but an almost continual bombardment of their goal was practically certain to result in a score. Allen again found the opening, and as the result of excellent judgment and a cool head scored the second all-important and deciding goal which won the Cup for Newcastle for the third time in their career.

His Majesty The King presented the Cup to the winners. Her Majesty The Queen also honoured the occasion by her presence.

Referee :—W. P. HARPER.

Result :—NEWCASTLE UNITED ... 2 goals.
ARSENAL ... ... 1 goal.

An Appreciation

FOR many of the details of the Cup Finals described in the preceding pages the Editor is indebted to the courtesy of the respective Editors of "The Times," "The Daily Telegraph," "The Sporting Chronicle," "Sporting Life," and "Athletic News," to whom he conveys his grateful acknowledg-
ments.

Issued by the Fruit Trades' Federations, Advertisement Department, 10—13, New Bridge Street, London, E.C.4

F.A. CUP FINALS 1882-1932 — TEAMS AND SCORERS

1883
BLACKBURN OLYMPIC 2 OLD ETONIANS 1 (aet).
Blackburn Olympic: Hacking, Ward, Warburton, Gibson, Astley, Hunter, Dewhurst, Matthews, Wilson, Crossley, Yates.
Old Etonians: Kinnaird, French, De Paravicini, Rawlinson, Foley, Chevallier, Anderson, Macauley, Goodhart, Dunn, Bainbridge.
Scorers: Matthews, Crosley; Goodhart.

1884
BLACKBURN ROVERS 2 QUEEN'S PARK (Glasgow) 1
Blackburn: Arthur, Beverley, Suter, McIntyre, J. Hargreaves, Forrest, Lofthouse, Douglas, Sowerbutts, Inglis, Brown.
Queen's Park: Gillespie, Arnott, MacDonald, Campbell, Gow, Anderson, Watt, Smith, Harrower, Allan, Christie
Scorers: Brown, Forrest; Christie

1885
BLACKBURN ROVERS 2 QUEEN'S PARK 0
Blackburn: Arthur, Turner, Suter, McIntyre, Haworth, Forrest, Lofthouse, Douglas, Brown, Fecitt, Sowerbutts
Queen's Park: Gillespie, Arnott, MacLeod, Campbell, MacDonald, Hamilton, Anderson, Sellar, Gray, McWhannel, Allan
Scorers: Forrest, Brown

1886
BLACKBURN ROVERS 0 WEST BROMWICH ALBION 0
Blackburn: Arthur, Turner, Suter, Douglas, Forrest, McIntyre, Heyes, Strachan, Brown, Fecitt, Sowerbutts.
WBA: Roberts, H. Green, H. Bell, Horton, Perry, Timmins, Woodhall, T. Green, Bayliss, Loach, G. Bell.
Replay:
BLACKBURN ROVERS 2 WEST BROMWICH ALBION 0
Blackburn: Walton for Heyes
WBA: Unchanged
Scorers: Brown, Sowerbutts

1887
ASTON VILLA 2 WEST BROMWICH ALBION 0
Aston Villa: Warner, Coulton, Simmonds, Yates, Dawson, Burton, Davis, Brown, Hunter, Vaughton, Hodgetts
WBA: Roberts, H. Green, Aldridge, Horton, Perry, Timmins, Woodhall, T. Green, Bayliss, Paddock, Pearson
Scorers: Hunter, Hodgetts

1888
WEST BROMWICH ALBION 2 PRESTON NORTH END 1
WBA: Roberts, Aldridge, H. Green, Horton, Perry, Timmins, Bassett, Woodhall, Bayliss, Wilson, Pearson
Preston N. End: Mills-Roberts, Howarth, N. Ross, Holmes, Russell, Graham, Gordon, J. Ross, J. Goodall, Dewhurst, Drummond
Scorers: Woodhall, Bayliss; Dewhurst.

1889
PRESTON NORTH END 3 WOLVERHAMPTON WANDERERS 0
Preston N End: Mills-Roberts, Howarth, Holmes, Drummond, Russell, Graham, Gordon, J. Ross, J. Goodall, Dewhurst, Thompson
Wolverhampton W. Baynton, Baugh, Mason, Fletcher, Allen, Lowder, Hunter, Wykes, Brodie, Wood, Knight
Scorers: Gordon, Goodall, Thompson

1890
BLACKBURN ROVERS 6 THE WEDNESDAY 1
Blackburn: Horne, James Southworth, Forbes, Barton, Dewar, Forrest, Lofthouse, Campbell, John Southworth, Walton, Townley
Wednesday: Smith, Brayshaw, Morley, Dungworth, Betts, Waller, Ingram, Woodhouse, Bennett, Mumford, Cawley
Scorers: Townley 3, Lofthouse, John Southworth, Walton; Bennett

1891
BLACKBURN ROVERS 3 NOTTS COUNTY 1
Blackburn: Pennington, Brandon, Forbes, Barton, Dewar, Forrest, Lofthouse, Walton, John Southworth, Hall, Townley
County: Thraves, Ferguson, Hendry, Osborne, Calderhead, Shelton, McGregor, McInnes, Oswald, Locker, Daft
Scorers: Southworth, Dewar, Townley; Oswald

1892
WEST BROMWICH ALBION 3 ASTON VILLA 0
WBA: Reader, Nicholson, McCulloch, Reynolds, Perry, Groves, Bassett, McLeod, Nicholls, Pearson, Geddes.
Villa: Warner, Evans, Cox, H. Devey, James Cowan, Baird, Athersmith, J. Devey, Dickson, Campbell, Hodgetts.
Scorers: Nicholls, Geddes, Reynolds

1893
WOLVERHAMPTON WANDERERS 1 EVERTON 0
Wolves: Rose, Baugh, Swift, Malpass, Allen, Kinsey, Topham, Wykes, Butcher, Wood, Griffin
Everton: Williams, Howarth, Kelso, Stewart, Holt, Boyle, Latta, Gordon, Maxwell, Chadwick, Milward
Scorer: Allen

1894

NOTTS COUNTY 4 BOLTON WANDERERS 1
County: Toone, Harper, Hendry, Bramley, Calderhead, Shelton, Watson, Donnelly, Logan, Bruce, Daft
Bolton: Sutcliffe, Somerville, Jones, Gardiner, Paton, Hughes, Dickinson, Wilson, Tannahill, Bentley, Cassidy
Scorers: Logan 3, Watson; Cassidy

1895

ASTON VILLA 1 WEST BROMWICH ALBION 0
Villa: Wilkes, Spencer, Welford, Reynolds, James Cowan, Russell, Athersmith, Chatt, J. Devey, Hodgetts, Smith
WBA: Reader, Williams, Horton, Taggart, Higgins, Perry, Bassett, McLeod, Richards, Hutchinson, Banks
Scorer: Devey

1896

THE WEDNESDAY 2 WOLVERHAMPTON WANDERERS 1
Wednesday: Massey, Earp, Langley, Brandon, Crawshaw, Petrie, Brash, Brady, Bell, Davis, Spiksley
Wolves: Tennant, Baugh, Dunn, Owen, Malpass, Griffiths, Tonks, Henderson, Beats, Wood, Black
Scorers: Spiksley 2; Black

1897

ASTON VILLA 3 EVERTON 2
Villa: Whitehouse, Spencer, Evans, Reynolds, James Cowan, Crabtree, Athersmith, J. Devey, Campbell, Wheldon, John Cowan
Everton: Menham, Meechem, Storrier, Boyle, Holt, Stewart, Taylor, Bell, Hartley, Chadwick, Milward
Scorers: Devey, Campbell, Crabtree; Bell, Hartley

1898

NOTTINGHAM FOREST 3 DERBY COUNTY 1
Forest: Allsop, Ritchie, Scott, Frank Forman, McPherson, Wragg, McInnes, Richards, Benbow, Capes, Spouncer
Derby: Fryer, Methven, Leiper, Cox, A. Goodall, Turner, J. Goodall, Bloomer, Boag, Stevenson, McQueen
Scorers: Capes 2, McPherson; Bloomer

1899

SHEFFIELD UNITED 4 DERBY COUNTY 1
United: Foulke, Thickett, Boyle, Johnson, Morren, Needham, Bennett, Beers, Hedley, Almond, Priest
Derby: Fryer, Methven, Staley, Cox, Paterson, May, Arkesden, Bloomer, Boag, McDonald, Allen
Scorers: Bennett, Priest, Beers, Almond; Boag

1900

BURY 4 SOUTHAMPTON 0
Bury: Thompson, Darroch, Davidson, Pray, Leeming, Ross, Richards, Wood, McLuckie, Sagar, Plant
Southampton: Robinson, Meehan, Durber, Meston, Chadwick, Petrie, Turner, Yates, Farrell, Wood, Milward
Scorers: McLuckie 2, Wood, Plant

1901

TOTTENHAM HOTSPUR 2 SHEFFIELD UNITED 2
Tottenham: Clawley, Erentz, Tait, Norris, Hughes, Jones, Smith, Cameron, Brown, Copeland, Kirwan.
United: Foulke, Thickett, Boyle, Johnson, Morren, Needham, Bennett, Field, Hedley, Priest, Lipsham
Scorers: Brown 2; Bennett, Priest
Replay:
TOTTENHAM HOTSPUR 3 SHEFFIELD UNITED 1
Tottenham: Unchanged
Sheffield United: Unchanged
Scorers: Cameron, Smith, Brown; Priest

1902

SHEFFIELD UNITED 1 SOUTHAMPTON 1
United: Foulke, Thickett, Boyle, Needham, Wilkinson, Johnson, Bennett, Common, Hedley, Priest, Lipsham
Southampton: Robinson, Fry, Molyneux, Meston, Bowman, Lee, A. Turner, Wood, Brown, Chadwick, J. Turner
Scorers: Common; Wood
Replay
SHEFFIELD UNITED 2 SOUTHAMPTON 1
Sheffield United: Barnes for Bennett
Southampton: Unchanged
Scorers: Hedley, Barnes, Brown

1903

BURY 6 DERBY COUNTY 0
Bury: Monteith, Lindsey, McEwen, Johnson, Thorpe, Ross, Richards, Wood, Sagar, Leeming, Plant
Derby: Fryer, Methven, Morris, Warren, A. Goodall, May, Warrington, York, Boag, Richards, Davis
Scorers: Leeming 2, Ross, Sagar, Plant, Wood

1904

MANCHESTER CITY 1 BOLTON WANDERERS 0
City: Hillman, McMahon, Burgess, Frost, Hynds, Ashworth, Meredith, Livingstone, Gillespie, A. Turnbull, Booth
Bolton: Davies, Brown, Struthers, Clifford, Greenhaigh, Freebairn, Stokes, Marsh, Yenson, White, Taylor
Scorer: Meredith

1905

ASTON VILLA 2 NEWCASTLE UNITED 0
Villa: George, Spencer, Miles, Pearson, Leake, Windmill, Brawn, Garratty, Hampton, Bache, Hall
Newcastle: Lawrence, McCombie, Carr, Gardner, Aitken, McWilliam, Rutherford, Howie, Appleyard, Veitch, Gosnell
Scorer: Hampton 2

1906

EVERTON 1 NEWCASTLE UNITED 0
Everton: Scott, W. Balmer, Crelly, Makepeace, Taylor, Abbott, Sharp, Bolton, Young, Settle, Hardman
Newcastle: Lawrence, McCombie, Carr, Gardner, Aitken, McWilliam, Rutherford, Howie, Veitch, Orr, Gosnell
Scorer: Young

1907

THE WEDNESDAY 2 EVERTON 1
Wednesday: Lyall, Layton, Burton, Brittleton, Crawshaw, Bartlett, Chapman, Bradshaw, Wilson, Stewart, Simpson
Everton: Scott, W. Balmer, R. Balmer, Makepeace, Tallor, Abbott, Sharp, Bolton, Young, Settle, Hardman
Scorers: Stewart, Simpson, Sharp

1908

WOLVERHAMPTON WANDERERS 3 NEWCASTLE UNITED 1
Wolves: Lunn, Jones, Collins, Hunt, Wooldridge, Bishop, Harrison, Shelton, Hedley, Radford, Pedley
Newcastle: Lawrence, McCracken, Pudan, Gardner, Veitch, McWilliam, Rutherford, Howie, Appleyard, Speedie, Wilson
Scorers: Hunt, Hedley, Harrison; Howie

1909

MANCHESTER UNITED 1 BRISTOL CITY 0
United: Moger, Stacey, Hayes, Duckworth, Roberts, Bell, Meredith, Halse, J. Turnbull, A. Turnbull, Wall
City: Clay, Annan, Cottle, Hanlin, Wedlock, Spear, Staniforth, Hardy, Gilligan, Burton, Hilton
Scorer: A. Turnbull

1910

NEWCASTLE UNITED 1 BARNSLEY 1
Newcastle: Lawrence, Whitson, Veitch, Low, McWilliam, Rutherford, Howie, Shepherd, Higgins, Wilson
Barnsley: Mearns, Downs, Ness, Glendinning, Boyle, Utley, Bartrop, Gadsby, Lilycrop, Tufnell, Forman
Scorers: Rutherford, Tufnell
Replay:
NEWCASTLE UNITED 2 BARNSLEY 0
Newcastle: Carr for Whitson
Barnsley: Unchanged
Scorer: Shepherd 2 (1 pen)

1911

BRADFORD CITY 0 NEWCASTLE UNITED 0
Bradford: Mellors, Campbell, Taylor, Robinson, Gildea, McDonald, Logan, Spiers, O'Rourke, Devine, Thompson
Newcastle: Lawrence, McCracken, Whitson, Veitch, Low, Willis, Rutherford, Jobey, Stewart, Higgins, Wilson
Replay
BRADFORD CITY 1 NEWCASTLE UNITED 0
Bradford City: Torrance for Gildea
Newcastle United: Unchanged
Scorer: Spiers

1912

BARNSLEY 0 WEST BROMWICH ALBION 0
Barnsley: Cooper, Downs, Taylor, Glendinning, Bratley, Utley, Bartrop, Tufnell, Lillycrop, Travers, Moore
WBA: Pearson, Cook, Pennington, Baddeley, Buck, McNeal, Jephcott, Wright, Pailor, Bowser, Shearman
Replay
BARNSLEY 1 WEST BROMWICH ALBION 0 (aet)
Barnsley: *Unchanged*
WBA: Unchanged
Scorer: Tufnell

1913

ASTON VILLA 1 SUNDERLAND 0
Villa: Hardy, Lyons, Weston, Barber, Harrop, Leach, Wallace, Halse, Hampton, Stephenson, Bache
Sunderland: Butler, Gladwin, Ness, Cuggy, Thompson, Low, Mordue, Buchan, Richardson, Holley, Martin
Scorer: Barber

1914

BURNLEY 1 LIVERPOOL 0
Burnley: Sewell, Bamford, Taylor, Halley, Boyle, Watson, Nesbit, Lindley, Freeman, Hodgson, Mosscrop
Liverpool: Campbell, Longworth, Pursell, Fairfoul, Ferguson, McKinlay, Sheldon, Metcalf, Miller, Lacey, Nicholl
Scorer: Freeman

1915

SHEFFIELD UNITED 3 CHELSEA 0
United: Gough, Cook, English, Sturgess, Brelsford, Utley, Simmons, Fazackerley, Kitchen, Masterman, Evans
Chelsea: Molyneux, Bettridge, Harrow, Taylor, Logan, Walker, Ford, Halse, Thompson, Croal, McNeil
Scorers: Simmons, Kitchen, Fazackerley

1920

ASTON VILLA 1 HUDDERSFIELD TOWN 0 (aet)
Villa: Hardy, Smart, Weston, Ducat, Barson, Moss, Wallace, Kirton, Walker, Stephenson, Dorrell
Huddersfield: Mutch, Wood, Bullock, Slade, Wilson, Watson, Richardson, Mann, Taylor, Swan, Islip
Scorer: Kirton

1921

TOTTENHAM HOTSPUR 1 WOLVERHAMPTON WANDERERS 0
Tottenham: Hunter, Clay, McDonald, Smith, Walters, Grimsdell, Banks, Seed, Cantrell, Bliss, Dimmock
Wolves: George, Woodward, Marshall, Gregory, Hodnett, Riley, Lea, Burrill, Edmonds, Potts, Brooks
Scorer: Dimmock

1922

HUDDERSFIELD TOWN 1 PRESTON NORTH END 0
Huddersfield: Mutch, Wood, Wadsworth, Slade, Wilson, Watson, Richardson, Mann, Islip, Stephenson, W.H. Smith
Preston N End: Mitchell, Hamilton, Doolan, Duxbury, McCall, Williamson, Rawlings, Jefferis, Roberts, Woodhouse, Quinn
Scorer: Smith (pen)

1923

BOLTON WANDERERS 2 WEST HAM UNITED 0
Bolton: Pym, Haworth, Finney, Nuttall, Seddon, Jennings, Butler, Jack, J.R. Smith, J. Smith, Vizard
West Ham: Hufton, Henderson, Young, Bishop, Kay, Tresardern, Richards, Brown, Watson, Moore, Ruffell
Scorers: Jack, J.R. Smith

1924

NEWCASTLE UNITED 2 ASTON VILLA 0
Newcastle: Bradley, Hampson, Hudspeth, Mooney, Spencer, Gibson, Low, Cowan, Harris, McDonald, Seymour
Villa: Jackson, Smart, Mort, Moss, Milne, Blackburn, York, Kirton, Capewell, Walker, Dorrell

1925

SHEFFIELD UNITED 1 CARDIFF CITY 0
United: Sutcliffe, Cook, Milton, Pantling, King, Green, Mercer, Boyle, Johnson, Gillespie, Tunstall
Cardiff: Farquharson, Nelson, Blair, Wake, Keenor, Hardy, W. Davies, Gill, Nicholson, Beadles, J. Evans
Scorer: Tunstall

1926

BOLTON WANDERERS 1 MANCHESTER CITY 0
Bolton: Pym, Haworth, Greenhalgh, Nuttall, Seddon, Jennings, Butler, Jack, J.R. Smith, J. Smith, Vizard
City: Goodchild, Cookson, McCloy, Pringle, Cowan, McMullan, Austin, Browell, Roberts, Johnson, Hicks
Scorer: Jack

1927

CARDIFF CITY 1 ARSENAL 0
Cardiff: Farquharson, Nelson, Watson, Keenor, Sloan, Hardy, Curtis, Irving, Ferguson, L. Davies, McLachlan
Arsenal: Lewis, Parker, Kennedy, Baker, Butler, John, Hulme, Buchan, Brain, Blyth, Hoar
Scorer: Ferguson

1928

BLACKBURN ROVERS 3 HUDDERSFIELD TOWN 1
Blackburn: Crawford, Hutton, Jones, Healless, Rankin, Campbell, Thornewell, Puddefoot, Roscamp, McLean, Rigby
Huddersfield: Mercer, Goodall, Barkas, Redfern, Wilson, Steele, Jackson, Kelly, Brown, Stephenson, W.H. Smith
Scorers: Roscamp 2, McLean; Jackson

1929

BOLTON WANDERERS 2 PORTSMOUTH 0
Bolton: Pym, Haworth, Finney, Kean, Seddon, Nuttall, Butler, McClelland, Blackmore, Gibson, W. Cook
Portsmouth: Gilfillan, Mackie, Bell, Nichol, McIlwaine, Thackeray, Forward, J. Smith, Weddle, Watson, F. Cook
Scorers: Butler, Blackmore

1930

ARSENAL 2 HUDDERSFIELD TOWN 0
Arsenal: Preedy, Parker, Hapgood, Baker, Seddon, John, Hulme, Jack, Lambert, James, Bastin
Huddersfield: Turner, Goodall, Spence, Naylor, Wilson, Campbell, Jackson, Kelly, Davies, Raw, W.H. Smith
Scorers: James, Lambert

1931

WEST BROMWICH ALBION 2 BIRMINGHAM 1
WBA: Pearson, Shaw, Trentham, Magee, W. Richardson, Edwards, Glidden, Carter, W.G. Richardson, Sandford, Wood
Birmingham: Hibbs, Liddell, Barkas, Cringan, Morrall, Leslie, Briggs, Crosbie, Bradford, Gregg, Curtis
Scorers: W.G. Richardson 2; Bradford

1932

NEWCASTLE UNITED 2 ARSENAL 1
Newcastle: McInroy, Nelson, Fairhurst, McKenzie, Davidson, Weaver, Boyd, Richardson, Allen, McMenemy, Lang
Arsenal: Moss, Parker, Hapgood, C. Jones, Roberts, Male, Hulme, Jack, Lambert, Bastin, John
Scorers: Allen 2; John

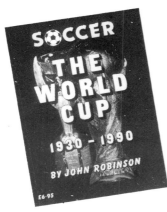

SOCCER —
THE
INTERNATIONAL
COMPETITIONS

Other publications from
Soccer Book
Publishing Ltd

THE EUROPEAN CHAMPIONSHIP 1958-1988
The definitive history of The European Nations Championship.

A 160 page book featuring ★ write-ups of each series ★ with full Country-by-Country statistical record of all games played ★ dates ★ scorers ★ half-times ★ attendances
SOFTBACK PRICE £5.95
HARDBACK PRICE £9.95
(postage £1.00 UK : £1.50 Overseas)

SOCCER — THE WORLD CUP 1930-1990
The complete history of Soccer's greatest competition.

Over 180 pages featuring ★ write-ups of each series ★ with full Country-by-Country record of Final Series Games ★ scorers ★ half-times ★ AND Statistics of every Qualifying game ..... thousands of results.
SOFTBACK PRICE £6.95
HARDBACK PRICE £10.95
(postage £1.25 UK : £1.75 Overseas)

Order direct from:
SOCCER BOOK PUBLISHING (Dept FAC)
72 St. Peters Avenue, Cleethorpes DN35 8HU, England

SPECIAL OFFER FOR BOTH ABOVE TITLES
SOFTBACK £10.00 : HARDBACK £15.00
(Postage £1.50 UK : £2.50 Overseas)